HOW TO TEACH

Commas, colons, connectives and conjunctions

Literacy

PHIL BEADLE

 Independent Thinking Press

First published by

Independent Thinking Press
Crown Buildings, Bancyfelin, Carmarthen, Wales, SA33 5ND, UK
www.independentthinkingpress.com

Independent Thinking Press is an imprint of Crown House Publishing Ltd.

First published 2015.

Photographs page 33 © olly - Fotolia.com, page 34 © olly - Fotolia.com, © Sylvie
Bouchard - Fotolia.com, page 112 © MarFot - Fotolia.com, page 139 © TristanBM -
Fotolia.com, © Timmary - Fotolia.com, © Dionisvera - Fotolia.com

Extracts from 'Table Talk: Brasserie Chavot, London, W1' by A. A. Gill © Times Newspapers Ltd, 2013 appears with kind permission
of The Sunday Times Magazine/News Syndication. Extract pages 80–81 is reproduced with the kind permission of Andrew Old.
Adaptation pages 94–95 and extract page 202 © Gary Wilson, 2008, Breaking through Barriers to Boys' Achievement: Developing a
Caring Masculinity, Network Continuum, is reproduced by permission of Bloomsbury Publishing Plc. Extract page 134 Department
for Children, Schools and Families, Support for Spelling. The National Strategies: Primary (London: DCSF, 2010) has been approved
under an Open Government Licence. Please visit: http://www.nationalarchives.gov.uk/doc/open-government-licence/version/3/.

British Library Cataloguing-in-Publication Data
A catalogue entry for this book is available
from the British Library.

Print ISBN 978-1-78135-128-4
Mobi ISBN 978-1-78135-178-9
ePub ISBN 978-1-78135-179-6
ePDF ISBN 978-1-78135-180-2

Printed and bound in the UK by
Gomer Press, Llandysul, Ceredigion

To my eldest genetic son, Leonard Joseph Beadle, who is the human on this planet I most wanted to meet, who I waited thirty-six years for, whose birth was the most transcendent moment of my life, who has never disappointed me, and whom I love as much as breathing.

And to Kevin McKellar, my first role model as a teacher, of whom not one of the thousands of children whose lives he touched would remember him as anything other than the kindest of saints, and who was taken when he still had decades of brilliance left.
A better man than me. RIP.

ACKNOWLEDGEMENTS

I have been lucky enough to meet so many absolutely wonderful people in the more recent years of my career; I think it would be remiss not to take the opportunity to thank them humbly for the friendship, the wine, the iconoclasm, the laughs, the cuddles and the truly excellent swearing.

The list of great people includes Paul Brown (an aesthete and a gent), Cris Campbell, Tait Coles, Rob Cooper (my best mate in England), David Didau (who, for a supposed apprentice, seems to be doing a scarily convincing impersonation of a master), Paul 'dog with two' Dix (proper respectable geezer), Ian Gilbert (mustard in a rumble), Nina Jackson (a sweetheart), Ben Kempka, all at Knox Grammar English department, Caroline Lenton (another sweetheart), Glen Maclachlan (my best mate in the Southern Hemisphere), Chris McPhee, Tony Minall, Tony O'Donohue, Martin Robinson (middle aged Cockney drama teachers in quality knitwear: be afraid world), Kevin Rowland, Steve Ruddy (Eaaagles!), Mr James Stafford, Ian Whitwham and the ribald high-priestess herself, Ros Wilson.

Special props must also go to my editor, Emma Tuck, who is the funniest person I have never met. And, most of all, I acknowledge the continued forbearance of the uberbabe, Jennifer Eirlys, without whose love I would have been someone else: someone far worse.

CONTENTS

PREFACE

At many points in this tome, you'll find there are instances when I have not obeyed my own advice; this is entirely deliberate. You'll find, for instance, that there are countless occasions on which I've *deliberately* put an adverb before a verb. In these cases I've *judiciously* weighed it up, and *definitely* felt I could *probably* cope with the slight jarring effect it *clearly* produces on the psyches of both reader and author. I also guide teachers not to allow their students to use capitals to display volume when there are a good few examples in the book of me doing the exact thing I'm briefing against. The reason for this is that, unlike your students, I am a partially functioning, independent adult who makes a meagre part of his living from writing. I am not seeking to impress examiners; I seek to entertain. My examiner is the reader, and if you have read one of my books before, you will know pretty well what you are going to get: an array of borderline inappropriate knob jokes stretched over an obviously spindly structural device, somehow fleshed out into a borderline cohesive narrative by the bludgeoning weight of the humour, that somehow, against the odds, teaches you loads of stuff you didn't know. I don't have to follow my own advice for teaching children how to write as I am not a child, and if I didn't already know all of the things in this book I wouldn't have been able to write it. I think there are also a couple of occasions where I use three exclamations together!!! I am allowed to do this because it is clear I am taking the mick. Children are not allowed to do this. You have to be in late middle age to get away with it.

I also need to warn you, as if you needed warning, about the 'appropriateness' (or not) of some of the humour. I am 49 years of age, have no interest whatsoever in the vagaries of social nicety and speak in my own voice, not some anthropologically esoteric academic code. Try not to be offended. If you are of the mind to try on that particular coat, and if anything in this book offends you to the point that you cannot take the information in it seriously, chuck it in the bin.

And let us now bring up a perspective about writing, and about the rules, that one must have some cognizance of in order to do it with any degree of skill: sometimes you've just got to go with the feel. That isn't to say that you should use going with the feel as an excuse for your ignorance of the rules. But once you have some command of them, then you can start subverting the rules deliberately to create interesting effects, both rhythmic and semantic. Rules are important, of course, and this book exists to help you understand them and then teach them to the young people who need access to them, but don't make a theocracy out of them. They exist to provide the structure within which we might play.

On a related tangent, it would be foolish of me to ignore the possibility that this book might be chanced upon in a branch of Oxfam by some petty grammarian who regards 'proper' grammar as having some moral aspect. Such people are responsible, as A. A. Gill – a writer who did not let his dyslexia hide his brilliance – notes, for, "The dullest, most pompous letters a paper gets ... from the grammar Stasi agent who has been reading *Eats, Shoots and* [*sic*] *Leaves* on the bog."[1] If you are one of those people and you spot the mistakes the proofreader has made in the proofing of this book – it's her fault, not mine, shoot her! – then any assertion that the author of this book is a symptom of what he is trying to cure has an interesting self-referential surrealism, but is really needless nit picking. Go back to your *Daily Mail*.

I am for the working class being held worthy of intellectual respect, and I am also for teaching children the stuff they need to know to attain this. I don't always get things right, as I am self-taught. My teachers didn't know this stuff, your teachers didn't know this stuff, and that is why this book

---

1   A. A. Gill, 'Table Talk: Brasserie Chavot, London, W1', *Sunday Times Magazine* (2 June 2013). See page 59 for how *sic* works.

is necessary. Ultimately, what it stands for is democracy: democratisation of expression, democratisation of some minor elegance in the written and spoken word, democratisation of having a voice. And it is a book that, while overly proud of its own anger, is also in possession of a pair of truisms that, for me, are not ever shouted loudly enough or with enough steel or violence of intent.

The first of these is the statement that literacy *is* political, and the second, built on the first, is that equipping children from the lower social orders with heavyweight skills of expression, when combined with teaching them their place in the hierarchy, is the most potently subversive political act available to any human.

It is my perspective that the most important thing you learn in school is how to communicate; and it is also my perspective that, systemically, we – the educators responsible for growing future generations that might use their literacy to fight the manifold punitive orthodoxies inflicted upon them – do not teach this very well. As a result, the rich children who are educated separately from ours are allowed to grow up with the sense that they alone have the erudition, the mastery and the skills of articulation to properly engage with any political arena. Furthermore, the elites have been indoctrinated to believe that they (somehow) have ownership of the language.

I will leave it to A. A. Gill, whose view of social class is radically different to that one might expect from a columnist in one of the 'top people's' papers, to point this out from the left bank of the inside. Speaking of the English language as an unstoppable river, he writes, "Nobody can alter its path of its destination, it belongs to whoever finds it in their mouth. It washes away dictionaries and lexicons and fun licking grammars. It is global and as free as breathing and the only truly democratic thing we own. Don't let anyone tell you that it's more theirs than yours because they don't dangle participles."[2]

---

2   Gill, 'Table Talk'.

Use this book to teach children to speak, to write, to read well. Use it to alter their destinies. Use it to teach them that there are rules, and they are worth learning. But, I repeat, don't make a theocracy out of them. And don't forget: to be properly nourishing, and to properly inspire, the line betwixt work and play should not always be immediately visible.

English always has been in a state of flux; there was no golden age when words and meaning matched, and the language stood firm and grand like mortarless rocks: words are born, live, decay and die – it's just the linguistic universe doing its stuff.

Julian Barnes, *Levels of Life* (2013)

INTRODUCTION

Once upon a time Kofi Annan delivered an inspirational speech about the importance of literacy. It was a good speech, and because it was a good speech people who had been paid to pontificate about reading and writing liked to quote it on occasion. Generally, when they did so, they'd edit out the ugly clang of statistics, so that, down to sixty-nine (or so) words, the meaning sang out as sweetly as an Al Green heartbreaker. And the chorus, it went:

> Literacy is a bridge from misery to hope … a bulwark against poverty … Literacy is a platform for democratization … It is an agent of family health and nutrition. For everyone, everywhere, literacy is, along with education in general, a basic human right. … Literacy is, finally, the road to human progress and the means through which every man, woman and child can realize his or her full potential.[1]

The problem with hook-line laden inspirational words delivered from behind a dais is that the form dictates that the audience is entertained, as inspirational words are only ever delivered for an audience, and are generally performed for either money or some other form of personal advancement. If we were to Ofsted Kofi Annan's view of literacy we might condense it to a checklist:

Breathtakingly audacious metaphors: tick.

Establishment of import of the subject: tick.

---

1   United Nations, 'Secretary-General Stresses Need for Political Will and Resources to Meet Challenge of Fight against Illiteracy' (press release, 8 September 1997). Available at: http://www.un.org/press/en/1997/19970904.SGSM6316.html/.

Reference to poor people to further establish importance of the subject and to emphasise the speaker's altruism: tick.

Appearing to really, really care about other's poverty while taking a tycoon's salary and dining regularly on lobster: tick.

Tick, tick, tick.

But do they really mean anything? Where does truth live here?

In 2007, I spent six months devoted almost entirely – except for a bestial week suffering food poisoning from having been force-fed a dog turd in a Belgian restaurant/sewagery[2] – filming a television series for Channel 4 called *Can't Read: Can't Write* that not even my mother watched.

The premise (or conceit) of the programme was that an idiot with a borderline personality disorder would take nine adult learners, all of whom had serious difficulties with literacy, and attempt to solve these with six months of blundering phonics lessons. Reality television permits little that is morally complicated or ambiguous – heroes, they save; villains, they rob – and, unambiguously, the heroes of this programme were the learners: inspiring people, whom I grew to admire, to like and to respect.

The teacher–student transaction is meant to be edifying for the student, but I took vastly more from these gentle people than I gave (and in some cases I taught them to read, which is not nothing). I learned from them.

I learned that Kofi Annan's words were not merely the empty rhetorical flourish of a career diplomat with an exalted position to protect; I learned that being born into my own family's compassion and work ethic was,

---

2   "Waiter, there is a dog turd in my moules-frites!"
"It is just something the mussel is eating, monsieur."

comparatively, a position of privilege; and, also, I learned ... that literacy *is* a bulwark against poverty.

This became apparent during an afternoon spent on a council estate at the very edge of West London, Feltham, on which two of the learners lived. After visiting Kelly, her spindly hall table groaning to the point of collapse beneath the weight of unopened bills piled upon it (there was no point in her opening them; she couldn't really read what they were asking her for), we filmed an inevitably narcissistic piece to camera on one of the few scrubby, litter strewn bits of green on the estate. "It's not the path to riches, low level literacy," I declaimed sadly, inarticulately and inadequately, an impotent epiphany dawning ...

The male learners on the course all worked for a living, and, with the exception of one, who (and very successfully) ran his own business, they all had the same job. A question for you, reader: what job can you do if you are male and you cannot read at all?[3]

A further thing I've noticed, from travelling around the country, is that often when you ask a cab driver outside of London for something they are unable to provide it. If, for instance, you ask a Birmingham cabbie to drive you to Birmingham University, or to a school that is on the same road as the cab rank, they won't have the first idea of how to get there,[4] and then when you request a receipt, they will often ask you to write it out yourself. In London, this practice is all about a bare-faced, though tacit, agreement between cabbie and punter that all tax is a ruling class scam, and that if we can both nick fifty pence off Her Majesty while she's looking the other way, then it's all good. Outside of the capital, the faces are often more shamed than they are

---

3   They were all bin men. Do not applaud yourself too loudly if you got this right. But respect your bin men.

4   "It's down the sodding road. Down. The. Sodding. Road. Oh, for God's sake. I'll walk."

bare: they will ask you to write it out yourself as they are unable to do so. Why do "working class kids get working class jobs"?[5]

Literacy *is* a bulwark against poverty.

I learned … that literacy *is* a platform for democratisation. The most interesting person I worked with on the series was Linda: an articulate woman with a lively mind who ran several successful businesses, lived in a beautifully appointed mews house near an Oxfordshire canal and who could read the words 'and', 'a' and 'it', but few others. The fact that her reading vocabulary had such little useful function did not stop her from being infatuated with literature to the extent that she kept a tended corner of her lovely front room as a library. It was populated predominantly by classics, and most days she would sit or kneel in that corner at some point, book open on her lap, inhaling deeply, poring over Shakespeare's sonnets, admiring the patterns, adoring the typeface, shedding heartbroken tears that she was unable to access their secrets. "What are they not telling me?" she asked on our first meeting, before etching the air with a voice that trembled with a deep, unrequited passion, and coughing out, "Like you need to breathe, I need to read!"[6]

One of the many fascinating insights that Linda shared was when, naively, I asked her why she thought the government did not pour a particularly impressive amount of hedge fund managers' tax cuts into resolving adult illiteracy. "It's obvious," she said. "We can't vote."

If you think with any stunted insight at all about the democratic process, you will realise it requires you to be literate to register a functional protest against the government that left you illiterate. If you cannot read, you will

---

5   Paul Willis, *Learning to Labor: How Working Class Kids Get Working Class Jobs* (New York: Columbia University Press, 1977).

6   Linda has been able to read perfectly well since winter 2007. Rather beautifully, I thought, the last time we met, she told Richard Madeley, on live telly, "I read a lot of rubbish, Richard. But at least I can tell it's rubbish."

not be able to tell the difference between the words 'Labour' and 'Conservative' on the ballot paper. If you cannot read, then you cannot even begin on the first tentative steps towards understanding what propaganda is, and that more or less everything you have ever been told is a lie designed to keep you cowed, obedient and controlled.

Literacy *is* a platform for democratisation.

I learned ... that literacy *is* an agent of family health and nutrition. One of the ladies on the course was called Teresa: she was (and is) a beautiful soul who'd brought up ten children, not all of whom were her own; and the kind of deeply empathetic person who is better than the rest of us, and who could not stand to see the suffering of a child (and she'd seen a lot of things no one should see and no child should ever experience) without doing something about it. Teresa was used to a full house, and to doing a lot of food shopping but, because she could not read, there were aspects of her weekly shop, aside from the obvious and really quite serious fiscal limits, that were difficult: if there wasn't a picture of the product on the tin, she couldn't buy it, as she wouldn't know what it was. This might seem small beer to you, but imagine having ten kids and only being able to purchase products that did not rely on you being able to read the label. It seems, perhaps, to you, like a passing bore. To someone who can't read, who has ten kids to feed, it was a weekly torture and a constant reminder of her own inabilities.

Literacy *is* an agent of family health and nutrition.

I learned ... that literacy *is* the road to human progress and the means through which every man, woman and child can realise his or her full potential.

I have been nervous about writing this book, and that is one of the reasons I have delighted to hear the charming swooshing sound of the deadline, as it has flown by on ~~three, four,~~ five separate occasions. The nervousness has existed for several reasons: because, despite the rigorous process of editing, there is an inevitability that there will be a typo or a grammatical error at some point in a book about literacy, and because I am going to have to tell the following story, and it is undeniably self-indulgent.

I understand if you want to skip this bit; but I was duty bound to write it because, as a functional metaphor for the transformative powers of literacy, there is no story I know better than my own: a mildly mythologised version of which might shed some light on what your commitment to improving the literacy skills of your students might achieve. It is the story of my mother, and the unintended consequences of a single teacher's actions.

My mother grew up in a town called Naas. It is twenty-five miles south-west of Dublin, in a county called Kildare. She has shown me the house in which she and her five siblings grew up: eight people lived behind its slanted front door and beneath the fractured roof that covered its paltry rooms. My grandfather was a part-time hospital porter at Naas General Hospital and, on occasion, a barman at the Curragh: a servant. Not, as the criminally underrated Irish writer Cathal Coughlan would have it, "just one more skill-free wetback with a liking for drink",[7] but a man whose qualities – those of extreme gentleness, a loving nature and a sense of humour at once both wicked and charming – were not necessarily those that were being asked for when decent remuneration was being handed out. The post-war Irish working class were poor in a way that we no longer properly understand the word, and my mother grew up in poverty without any real knowledge that she was doing so. The only time there was any spare money in the house was when the rich English people came over to spend theirs drinking and betting on horses, and would occasionally condescend to giving Granddad a tip for his work behind the bar.

Mum has since shown me the branches in which she would occasionally find stray chicken eggs, delighting her own mother when she brought them

---

7   Cathal Coughlan, 'Eerin Go Braghag', from the album *Grand Necropolitan* (Kitchenware Records, 1996).

home. She has talked of the time when she stopped Granddad shooting a rabbit, thereby condemning the family to an evening without meat. And has talked to me, without any tangible regret, about a happy childhood in which hunger existed as something more concrete and more gnawing than as a plausible metaphor for ambition.

Granddad lost his job at the hospital and could not find other work. His eldest son, my Uncle Christie, had already left Naas' wet, grey skies for the adulterated promise of England, so Granddad, leaving his wife and five of his kids back in Kildare, travelled to England to find whatever employment was available to him. He promised them that if he hadn't sent for them in three weeks, then he'd return home, and was as good as his word. He obtained a job as a porter in Bethlem Royal Hospital, and the family settled in an unpromising area of South London. There my mother met my father: they married in their teens, and the week before Mum was twenty, she gave birth to the child who has written this book.

My siblings and I grew up on what is now an expensive and sought after estate of small houses, but was then only ever perceived as being a first step on the ladder. It was, and is, called the Alexandra Estate, and, until recently, carried a brass plaque from when it was built which described the estate as providing housing – these are the exact words, "For the hard-working poor."[8]

My story is the story of a teacher's intervention.

In what is now known as Year 10, but was then the fourth year, I was sitting wasting time in the DT block, when a teacher who I very much respected saw me reading *The Sun*, and was made angry by it. This teacher had, I think, noticed that my accent was not the same as the other boys' in the top set, and had, I think, seen past my flippancy. I felt his anger like an emotional assault, and was partially broken by it: he was a gentle (though strong) man

---

8   The plaque is no longer there. It was nicked and, in all probability, melted down by members of the rather less hard-working poor.

not given to needless displays of rage. But seeing the child I was (am) reading *The Sun* inflamed something inside of him, and, whilst still very much controlled, he gave voice to a political rage that he usually carried in a more silent way. "You are a clever boy, Phil," he said kindly, but not without menace. "Why are you reading that?"

I liked this teacher. I respected him. I was a little scared of him. I stuttered in reply, "Because of the football, Sir. Crystal Palace. South-east London. Football, Sir. Not ladies' bosoms, Sir. No, not at all, not bosoms, Sir. Football, Sir. Crystal Palace: the Eagles. Selhurst." I can't remember exactly what I said. But I do remember the crippling teenage embarrassment at having been rumbled.

"You are too clever to be reading that," he said from behind an elegantly cropped goatee beard, his one stud earring signalling something half profound and a quarter important. "Tomorrow, I will bring you in a newspaper. Do you promise you'll read it?"

I promised.

The next day he brought me in one of the big newspapers that posh people read. I'd seen one of these before. Nicholas, who I knew then as the school swot and as a pariah in a community in which football eclipsed learning, ambition or kindness, and who I now realise was probably the best of us, had once shown me his copy of *The Times*. It had a section entitled 'Broadcasting Guide' where the 'TV Guide' should have been, and I had therefore, quite rationally, written the organ off as being irredeemably pretentious. I was aware that posh people read big newspapers, but didn't really know there were different varieties. The one my teacher gave me was called *The Guardian*, which is a silly name for a paper (until you think about it).

As I respected the teacher, I did read the newspaper he gave to me the next morning. I didn't understand all of it, and focused predominantly on the sports pages, but I did read it. The day after he asked me what I thought.

"There's a lot more writing in the posh people's papers, isn't there, Sir? If you look at *The Sun*, there's more pictures. It's almost as if the people who make *The Sun* think their readers are a bit stupid."

"Yes ..."

"And I read that paper every day. Does that make me stupid?"

" ..."

"Does it? Do the people who write it want us to be stupid, Sir? Is that what it's for? To keep people like me stupid?"

"Shall I bring *The Guardian* in for you tomorrow?"

"Yes, Sir. Please, Sir. I'll read it again."

And he did. And I read it. And this teacher with the earring, who probably does not remember that he ever taught me, and who would not even remember my name if he heard it, brought in this newspaper sometimes.

It was an infinitesimally small gesture from a teacher – a gesture that cost him little, if anything (as I realise now he was just dumping his old copy on me, as the crosswords were always half done) – towards developing the literacy of a working class half male. But that long forgotten act from decades ago has ricocheted off the walls as I've stumbled through life; it sits on my shoulder this evening, smiling benignly, as I tap away at my ninth book; and it smiles in a vastly more sanguine and mature manner than it used to do when it was wetting itself with glee for the nine years I spent filing columns on government education policy for the very newspaper my teacher once offered me as a toehold into a world I might, one day, possibly, understand.

It does me little credit hoisting my own upbringing as a flag for working class achievement, I know (and I am genuinely apologetic here), but I think there is the shadow of a kernel of a half metaphor here that is sufficiently worthwhile to make you, dear teacher, angry enough to get rigorous about literacy. Without the intervention of that teacher I might have been a labourer, an electrician, a failed bantamweight, a pub bore, a minor larcenist, an insurance clerk in an office above a second class pizza establishment on a suburban high street. With their help I have, instead, been a minor irritant to a series of education secretaries; I have authored several partially readable books which have remained partially readable when translated into Slovenian, Chinese, Polish, Latvian, etc.; I have met Kim from *How Clean Is Your House* and, indeed, Aggie too; I have walked into bars in rural Australia and been told by the barman that I looked a bit like Phil Beadle (only much older); I have found myself in a hotel room with David Soul at 3.30 a.m. drinking rank sherry that leered at us from a crystal decanter, discussing what a good King Lear he would make; and, finally and most importantly, I have taken my mother back to Ireland, for my first ever visit, at the age of 42, to the land of half of my culture and half of my heritage.

And here is the denouement: my first ever time in my mother's home country was not as a barman, a hospital porter, nor as any kind of servant. No. My first time in my mother's home country was for a speaking engagement at the castle in the centre of Dublin, as a warm-up act for the President of Ireland, Mary McAleese, who was aware of my work, had requested my presence and to whom my Mum was introduced.

And I have stood, the next day, at my grandfather's graveside in Bawdenstown, and witnessed Mum talking to his gravestone: "You used to ask me, 'What, in God's name, are you *educatin'* that boy for?' You know now, Daddy. You know now."

Literacy *is* the road to human progress and the means through which every man, woman and child can realise his or her full potential.

The way out of the ghetto is not boxing, nor indeed any form of violence, and it is not football, nor indeed any form of codified violence. These will keep you in the ghetto, and these will keep you stupid. The way out of whatever ghetto you have been raised in, be it a "council estate of the mind", be it a physical ghetto or be it philosophical, is reading; and the way out of the ghetto is writing. And if you can get really good at reading and writing, then you have a voice. And when you have a voice you can use it. You can sculpt missiles of metaphorical spit into unruly perfection before hurling them at the milky visages of the "heifer-faced Etonians and Ivy Leaguers"[9] whose tribe profit from keeping you in the ghetto. You can tell them you see through the methods of institutionalised social control (the newspapers, the pub, football and the Church) that are used to keep you, and the likes of you, not only stupid and poor but grateful for being stupid and poor. And what is more, you can challenge them in the language they claim to own, thereby proving that they don't, and that their claim to intellectual superiority is a work of fantasy worthy of the mind of Lewis Carroll, and you can prove that their right to rule is a temporary historical glitch. If you can read and write you no longer have to be deferent to your oppressors. If you can read and write you don't have to beg any more; you can take what you want from life.

Literacy, for working class people, is a matter of life and death: it is the path away from the black economy and the hand-to-mouth existence that condemns millions of decent people to lives of misery and debt. With literacy, you can fight the policy makers who have never seen close up what poverty can do to humans, who legislate to increase it, who seek to put its victims under a pathologising microscope and then blame them for some innate, probably genetic, failing; when the failing has been inflicted upon them by politics and by circumstance.

With literacy you can articulate your anger.

---

9   Cathal Coughlan and The Grand Necropolitan Quartet, 'Shipman Memorial', from the album *Rancho Tetrahedron* (Kitchenware Records, 2010).

As such, and out of respect for it being the path to human progress, I would argue that it is a political and moral responsibility to equip children with it as well as you are able. If you are going to teach children to write, then teach them how to write as well as it is possible to do it. They will respond to your expectations. (Write yourself, and get better at it by doing it regularly. Report what you have learned about the craft of it in the next lesson.) If you are not going to do this with the degree of political seriousness it requires, then don't bother doing it at all. Get a job in the dry cleaners instead. We need better than you.

One of Kofi Annan's statements about literacy is that it is a "basic human right". If we take a look at Maslow's hierarchy of needs, literacy can get you all of them (except breathing and excretion, which tend to happen without the aid of improving books). It can be the basis of supplying most of your physiological needs: it can get you food, water and sometimes (often) sex; it can win you sleep in a comfortable bed; it can keep you safe and win you love; it can earn you the respect of others and respect for yourself; it can enter you into the realms of political and moral understanding in which you might play, exercise the muscles in your head and become ... all of the things you could, one day, with effort, possibly be.

If we are to acknowledge its importance, its primal and transcendental nature, its transformational powers, then we must ask a question, which comes with a qualification. "Alright, I can acknowledge this stuff is important. But whose job is it? Surely it's not mine. I teach DT for God's sake."

It's your job.

My friend Tony, a Nigerian man, who is degree level qualified as an accountant, but who, because of the casual racism endemic in this country, is a cab driver, and who, for his imagined sins, spends a greater proportion of his life than he would like driving people around who are nowhere near as intelligent, hardworking nor as moral as he, has a series of homespun Nigerian phrases which he is prone to trotting out on an early morning when the light will not be up for three hours and the cold bites harsh, and – yes! – we're off to Bury St Edmunds. The best of these, should you ask him how far he is from paying off his mortgage, is the glumly expressed, dismissive monotone of, "Frog has no tail." He delivers this grumpily from beneath tired eyebrows, and it remains impenetrable even after he's explained it. "You don't ask a frog about his tail; frog hasn't got a tail. Don't ask me about paying off the mortgage; frog has no tail." He also tells me, "When a tiger comes into the village and eats a leper, everyone says, 'Thank God. Evil has left the village.' But when, the next day, a tiger comes into the village and eats the king's son, people say, 'My God! Evil has come to the village.'" I don't understand this either, but it doesn't stop me liking it.

Another of Tony's favourite mutterings on the subject of villages is, "It is the village that educates the child." I think the meaning here is that kids' education is the corporate responsibility of a whole community.

If we can start with the basic assumption that literacy is, in Annan's words, a basic human right, and that it is the village's responsibility to ensure that all children have access to this basic human right, then whose job is it? It is everyone's, of course: the parents', the cleaners', the maths teachers' and the English teachers' too.

Whilst you can certainly understand a maths teacher thinking that making spurious links to literacy during a lesson on algebra is a waste of their time, effort and skills, as they have their own literacy – numeracy: literacy in a whole other language – and whilst you can empathise with teachers in other subject areas who might feel that maintaining the integrity of their subject related content is the most important part of their job, and who probably don't get the amount of hours on the timetable that they feel they need to cover the syllabus, the fact remains that literacy is the only subject that is perceived as being a human right. It is the subject that infiltrates all other subjects. It is the basic skill on which nigh all other skills in the curriculum are dependent, or as I read in the first teaching book I ever encountered, "a quicksilver among metals – mobile, living and elusive".[10]

If institutions want to do something serious about improving the literacy outcomes of their students, they must confront the barriers to their students attaining more. My intention with this book is to outline some of those barriers and to come up with a series of approaches and/or ideas that might help you on your journey towards being a transformational agent in terms of your effect on your students' skills.

The first and most important thing that any institution (or teacher) will have to do, if it is remotely serious about making a move towards being transformational, is to look at itself and to confront something that is uncomfortable for any educational institution: the issue of teacher knowledge. The first thing you will have to change is you.

---

10 John Dixon, *Growth through English: A Report Based on the Dartmouth Seminar 1966* (Reading: National Association for the Teaching of English, 1969), p. 1.

POOR LITERACY SKILLS AMONGST TEACHERS (PARTICULARLY IN TERMS OF THEIR UNDERSTANDING OF PUNCTUATION)

We have all been in the situation where we have gone to our pigeonhole and taken out a written communication from a colleague, and pondered, grimly exhaling, as we've intoned, "Sheesh! I really like _____, but should he/she really be a teacher?" Likewise, those of you who are parents may well receive weekly newsletters from your child's school, and might possibly have noted, regularly and ruefully, every Friday, that the writer of the newsletter and the possessive apostrophe may never have been that close at any time, but are clearly significantly estranged now.

It is understandable how this has happened. In many ways teaching, an impossible job with endless hours, is not something you would recommend to 'high quality' graduates who could command vastly better salaries working for commercial firms. Consequently, prior to the import of some of the 'Teach Firsters' who have saved education from itself, most teachers were as thick as two particularly rotund Cuban cigars on a fat day, and as dull witted as a partially redeemable masonry nail. This is further compounded by the fact that not all teachers are English teachers. Some have other specialisms.

As a result, the carpentry teacher, who may well be a really bloody good carpenter, is not necessarily wildly nuanced in his use of the semicolon.

Fair enough.

But it doesn't help the poor child, desperate to learn how to write, when some of his teachers are not really able to do so with any particular fluency or knowledge of the rules themselves.

POPPING THE FALLACIES

There is another very serious issue, which is the amount of really damaging wrong information in teachers' heads that they blithely pass on to students. This is not the fault of the teachers or the students. Teachers were, themselves, taught stuff about literacy by their own teachers that was (and remains) patently untrue, and they have seen no reason to question it. But there are various 'rules' that have hung around like the stench of fear at an abattoir, and these 'rules' have made a decent contribution to messing up a lot of children's ability to write.

By way of an insight into the problem, I'm going to ask you to take a wild, imaginative leap and imagine that the writer of this book is 11 years of age in something other than emotional maturity; I am new at secondary school, and have really, really tried really, really hard, and lots of really, really lovely teachers at my primary school have done their absolute best to help me, but I just can't work out where the full stop goes, and all I want is a rule to help me, that's all I want, please can you help me, please can you define a sentence, to help me stop writing sentences that are over seventy words long, life at school would be so much easier if I had a simple rule I could apply, does it go here, because I think I've prob'ly finished what I wanted to say

Can you come up with a watertight rule that defines where the full stop goes for an 11-year-old, level 2 learner? Have a go. See if you can do it. What, exactly, is a sentence?

Here are some answers:

- *A sentence must make sense.* No, it mustn't. I'll get my 10-year-old son to explain: "My Dad certainly doesn't make any sense at all after he's come back from the pub with Martin Robinson. He speaks in sentences about how much he trucking gloves us, but they don't actually make any sense at all. Maybe they're just fragments." The boy is right, of course: some really hyperactive sentences nestle like a broken alliterative cup fox aside the jam jar and wardrobe of jismy meaning. They don't necessarily make any real sense. They're still sentences.

- *A sentence must have a clause.* I'm sorry. I'm only 11, but I find the notion of clauses to be somewhat too abstract. It's a rule I want.

- *A sentence must have a subject, a verb and an object.* No.

The point in asking this question is not to make you feel daft: it is to fess up. I've never been a clever enough teacher to help this kid. All he wants is a rule, and I can't provide it for him. The best I've done so far is to teach him what a verb is, and to tell him a sentence has to have one (unless it is direct speech, in which case any old fragment will do, or you are trying on the groove of a GCSE version of style where the one word sentence is king). I've got nothing better, and I continue to fail him. I've found that with the kids who can't get anywhere near an accurate full stop, getting them to identify what a pronoun is, and then putting the full stop directly before it, has some vague traction as an idea to help them to a first understanding of how things work.

But other than this, I've been pretty useless to needy kids of this variety over a twenty year teaching career.[1]

The aim here is to identify something quite important about literacy: some of the skills that we take for granted as adults – every reader of this book can place a full stop correctly, I'd hope – are actually way more difficult to define than we think. It's one thing being able to do something yourself, it's another being able to teach it.

Let's try another one. Where do you put a comma?

(Deliberate pause for slightly too arch ironic effect)

If your immediate response to this question is to reach in the direction of the pause,

(Deliberate pause for self-referential, ironic effect)

or the breath,

(Deliberate pause for repetitive, self-referential, ironic effect)

then don't be embarrassed: you are no less well-educated than about 80 per cent of secondary school teachers, and thankfully very few primary teachers. (Honest!)

But if you learn nothing else from this book, learn this: you do not put a comma where you want to take a breath! It is an absurdity that teachers perpetrate because they haven't actually thought about things. What if you

---

1   However, since writing this, I've been in the presence of a genius: a gentleman from Chichester College, who says that he teaches it by getting the young person to put a full stop after every seventh word, and then gets them to read their work out loud and see if there is a better place to put it. This works because, in truth, the full stop does come after you have finished what you were going to say, and it is related to the rhythmic fall of the cadence.

want to take, the, breath in entirely the wrong place? What, if, you've, just, recently, been, running?

There are rules here. None of them are as esoteric, as abstract or as absurd as putting a punctuation mark at the exact point in a sentence that an involuntary bodily function manifests. If the 'put a comma when you want to take a breath' rule worked, then there would be a notable difference between the frequency of commas used in each sentence according to the altitude at which it was written: Dutch and Belgian writers would fill books with lengthy parades of comma free sentences, and you'd never get anywhere reading a book by any member of the Quito school of magic realists, as there'd be almost no words to speak of ... breathlessly ,,, just a series of commas.

The early years of my own education came with the 'enrichment' of what my brother and I came to know as 'Saturday morning suffering' at the hands of nuns, many of whom resembled walnuts that had been stored for decades in a particularly voracious pickling oil. I recall one Saturday morning in Sister Dimpnah's class, at the age of 7, while everyone else of my age was watching Noel Edmonds' *Multi-Coloured Swap Shop*, asking her where you put a comma.

Sister was certain of many things that were and are palpably gibberish. Her answer was (initially, at least) confident.

"Ah, sure now, Philip, you use a comma when you want to take a pause."

I probed the nun.

"When do you use a colon, then?"

"Ah, well now, dat's when you want to take a bigger pause."

"What about a semicolon?"

"Sure! Dat's a grand big pause dere now, Phil: the semicolon ..."

We did not get on to the full stop, as even then I found it a chasteningly difficult thing to either explain or to understand. But a realisation dawned on me at the age of 7: she doesn't know! She's not telling the truth! My teacher is telling me a fib! (God, that must mean that apples are actually good for you,[2] and that Sister Dimpnah isn't personally married to Jesus.)

HOW THE SISTER DIMPNAH JUSTIFICATION CAME ABOUT

Strap yourself in reader. Here is a poem about punctuation that I got from reading Lynne Truss, and though it is two grades down from exciting, it illustrates a point.

> The stops point out, with truth, the time of pause
> A sentence doth require at ev'ry clause.
> At ev'ry comma, stop while *one* you count;
> At semicolon, *two* is the amount;
> A colon doth require the time of *three*;
> The period *four*, as learned men agree.[3]

When you ask teachers to analyse this, and to come to some understanding of how the 'use a comma to take a pause' nonsense came about, there's generally a member of the English department who is uncomfortable with having their faulty belief system overturned by an overpaid consultant/idiot, and who will immediately come up with something like, "Ooo. Ooo. Ooo. Ooo. You are the fakest of fake gurus. You just made a clanking bastard of an

---

2   I'm not sure this joke works. I wonder whether I am trying too hard to show how clever I am here.
3   Lynne Truss, *Eats, Shoots & Leaves: The Zero Tolerance Approach to Punctuation* (London: Profile Books, 2003), pp. 112–113.

error: you said that you don't use a comma when you want to take a pause, and this is saying that you use a comma when you want to take a pause. I should be in your position because you are a rubbishy hypocrite and I am the epitome of English teaching excellence!"

I wait for this anger to blow out, as this teacher is unable to tell the difference between reading and writing (which you would have thought was a fairly easy thing to work out, particularly for an English teacher). What the poem explains are the rules for readers. It does not tell you the rules for writers. It does not tell you where you put the comma. Reading and writing are not the same thing, you see.

An explanation: reading and writing are often confused, and are perceived to be interlinked or mutually dependent. They are, of course, as you can't write before you can read a bit. But while it would be rash to say that the relationship between reading and writing is a little less intimate than many teachers or children's authors would have it, and whilst it would also be rash to say that reading a lot does not automatically make you a better writer, it might also be true. Reading and writing are separate skills using the same code. One is the process of decoding meaning from a set of signs, the other a process of encoding it with the same signs. Consequently, as distinct disciplines they have entirely distinct rules. As such, the rule for what comma usage signifies to someone going through the process of reading, taking meaning from the code, is distinct from where you place the comma when you are writing, placing meaning into code. So, yes, you do take a pause, a rest, a break, a short nap (even) when you are reading and chance upon a little cat's chin shaped squiggle perching on the line directly after a word; but you do not conflate this rule with the rules for commas when you are writing, because encoding and decoding, though complementary, are (kind of) opposite processes.

Sister Dimpnah also taught me something else regarding punctuation that you will have been taught too, which is equally complete rubbish, and that you may even still believe after I have told you that it is a crock. Sister assured me – and this was a certainty as certain as the fact that unbaptised babies sat in limbo counting their sins for all eternity, and that the Assumption of Mary was really, truly, formally accepted as holy dogma by the Catholic Church before the 1950s[4] – that there was one place, sure as hell(!), that if you put a comma before it, well, then it wasn't a mortal sin (you wouldn't actually go to hell if you did it), but it was certainly a sin of the venal variety, and, should you commit it, you'd have to atone by spending an ample amount of time in a small, dark room with a man who had never, ever had sex (allegedly). You too were probably taught that there was one word that you must never, ever, not ever, never, never, never, ever, ever, not even once, never, not even once, never, not even once – I mean – never, never. Never ... ever put a comma before, and that word was ... 'and'.

It's nonsense, of course.

You can put a comma before 'and'.

All the best writers do.

Charles Dickens puts a comma before 'and'.

Martin Amis does. His Dad too. Julian Barnes puts a comma before 'and'. Christopher Hitchens, the great non-fiction prose stylist of recent generations, puts a comma before 'and', and if it's alright for them, then it's alright for the kids that you (or I) teach. 'And' is a coordinating conjunction. You can put commas before them.

---

4   "The doctrine of the immaculate conception was announced or discovered by Rome in 1852, and the dogma of the Assumption in 1951. To say that something is 'man-made' is not always to say that it is stupid." Christopher Hitchens, *God is not Great: The Case against Religion* (London: Atlantic Books, 2007), p. 117.

WRITING IS MUSIC!

My favourite teacher at school, Mr Latham, said something to me (probably vastly less often than I recall him doing so) that I couldn't understand. He would utter, "Writing is just music really, Phil." Mr Latham was a great bloke and a smashing teacher, so I wanted to understand what he meant by this; and I tried to understand what he meant by this; but wasn't able to. I understood that poetry and lyrics were not the same thing (even at the age of 14 I knew the scansion in a lyric was different to that in a poem), but couldn't groove to the idea of the two art forms I most liked being somehow synaesthesic. I could see how they could combine to create something greater than the sum of the parts, and could just about tell the difference between a clever song and one written to entertain people with low expectations. I could also spot lyrical pretension; I had heard my own attempts at song writing. But it was too big a jump so see (or hear or feel) that writing and music were the same.

Nowadays, after much work and many years, I understand what Mr Latham meant. Writing really is, in many ways, merely music ... restrained. To give you a way into this, reader, a question: who do you, personally, think was the greatest artistic genius of the twentieth century?

Don't write your answer in this gap.

This question was a zero sum game. There is a right answer and, by implication, a near infinity of wrong ones. The correct answers are as follows, and in reverse order:

In third place – Daniel Corbett, the BBC weatherman[5]

In second place – Sir Sidney James

And first – Stevie Wonder

The stereotypical response to the 'Who was the greatest artistic genius of the twentieth century?' question is to grope in the direction of a dauber (Picasso or Dali) or a wordsmith (Beckett, or perhaps even Lorca if you are trying to show off how intellectually trendy you are). But all these artists were but mere monotone amateurs in comparison to Stevland Hardaway Morris. In the mid-1970s, Stevie Wonder made music so good that one could ignore the fact that the words were generally, with a few marginal exceptions, hippy

---

5   Daniel's moment in the sun seems to have passed, but as Neil Young sang, "It is better to burn out than fade away," and Corbett burns brightly! It may be that you are one of the many unlucky ones who never got to see him at the peak of his powers and fame; if you are ignorant of his work, he was the weathercaster's answer to Paul Gascoigne. In the same way that Gascoigne has made all other Englishmen's attempts at playing the futile game appear laughable by comparison, Corbett makes all other weathercasters appear risible amateurs when stood beside the master. If you doubt this, go on to YouTube and see weathercasting as it should be done.

Initially, you will note that you just really like him. Then, soon enough, your attention will be drawn to the fact that he manages to make a brief mention of snow over the Mendips somehow Shakespearean, and the fact that, as his exquisite cadence and range float over the words, his hands perform a ballet so entrancing, so eloquent, that he is either the greatest natural talent weathercasting has unfairly neglected, or that he puts more man hours into choreographing and rehearsing his 'improvisation' than even Eddie Izzard does. By the end you will be entranced, wishing you had recorded the weather forecast. But Dan has more! He would end every single broadcast with the recurring motif of, "That's the weather ... for now." And smile casually, knowingly, ironically: a master of the art form satirising that very form while, at the same time, doing it better than anyone else has ever done it. You can't fake genius. It lives entirely outside of conventional methods and judgements.

drivel. The reason one could ignore the gaucheness of the lyrics was that Stevie's music, certainly in its golden period (before the disappointing debacle of 'I Just Called to Say I Love You' when the world caved in and nothing was certain any more), was a sublime synthesis of melody and rhythm. In his pomp, Stevie appeared to have been gifted melodies by high ranking angels, and was somehow able to combine these with a rhythmic sensibility that you might easily imagine Beelzebub, surrounded by willing ladies, grooving to in a nightclub with the reddest of lighting.

There is a point to this.

When working with students on improving their writing, I tell them, "Writing is just music, really." And I watch their faces ghost over with confusion. "I want to understand what you mean by this, Sir; and I have tried to understand what you mean by this; but I am unable to." And they stay glazed and confused until I ask them a question, "What are the two fundamental elements of music that make it music as opposed to, say, speech?" Initially, on being asked this question, the two musical qualities exhibited by the students are umming and errming, until such point as one bright spark says, "Rhythm!" And they are right. And I congratulate them. And then look for other ideas.

It can take much longer to get someone to say melody. (I am aware that I am playing 'guess what's in the teacher's head' here, so award any interesting thought, but I am looking for a specific answer.) I will ask students the question, "If writing is music, then which element of writing plays the melody and which plays the rhythm?" The correct response eventually appears. To really get kids to understand the importance of punctuation the music analogy is useful. If they can come to some appreciation that, to be truly great, contemporary music has to have a groove, and that writing is, somehow, a related art form, then they can come to respect the chief purveyors of the rhythm: punctuation and sentence length.[6]

Music is an advanced form of mathematics; the rhythmic elements of writing are similar: they are in the arena of number. If you cannot master the maths, then the writing may well be partially melodic (it may make relatively interesting pictures in a reader's head, if they can be bothered to get through the rhythmic sludge they have to trudge through in order to access it), but without rhythm it will never make you want to dance; nor will it properly upset your parents; and it won't not make you want to have sex; and it will not be the all-encompassing sensual pleasure in either construction or consumption that it has the potential to be.

To overextend the musical analogy, there is a song by Kate Bush called 'Sat in Your Lap', which sits on her most esoteric and perhaps most interesting long player, *The Dreaming*. The drumming in this song is particularly interesting as Kate banned her drummer from using the full kit. Normally, most drum patterns in non-classical music are based around the bass drum (thud), the snare drum (crack), the hi-hat (tchika, tchika, tchika), the toms (rat-tat-tat) and the cymbals (which crash). Kate forbade her drummer from using the cymbals, hi-hat and snare for this song, forcing him to work with a restricted palette.[7] It's a sonically and rhythmically interesting piece, but you wouldn't want to listen to it all day as its rhythmic monotony would do your head in; neither would you want to listen to a whole album of it. This is what it's like reading the writing of a student that contains only full stops, wrongly applied commas and the odd question mark: like seeing painting after painting which feature only blue and green, and an eccentrically placed smudge of orange. There's a full palette of rhythmic effects and experiments available to the writer who uses all the tools of writing that have been made available to them. It's a shame and a waste to play a song with only one drum.

---

6   Syllables are important too. But they are too complicated for this book.
7   Listen to it. It's here: http://www.youtube.com/watch?v=xEVMfG8z490/.

LEARN THE RULES OF PUNCTUATION; TEACH THEM TO THE KIDS

I have spent a lot of time doing this. When I work with a new class, punctuation is the first thing I ever teach them, and they are always made a little angry by it. Given that the calls for my services as a teacher come only when a school realises that their English results may be the root cause of really nice, dedicated people losing their jobs, I am generally only required to work with Year 11s. Sometimes, I am brought in to help out rather late in the day. I rapidly run through the rules of punctuation with these 16-year-olds, perhaps a month (or even a week) before their 'terminal' exams, and the reaction from the kids is always the same: "Shouldn't we (perhaps) have been taught this before?"

It does not even necessarily matter what sector we are dealing with: primary, secondary or FE. In my admittedly individual and anecdotal experience, I have never met a single student who had possession of the full gamut of rules for punctuation. This applies to many teachers too. When I do the full day's CPD that this book is merely a marginally linguistically more sophisticated transcript of, there are palpable sighs of relief that a concern a teacher may have carried around with them for decades – the fact that they don't know the first thing about punctuation – can now be resolved without them ever having to admit the fact that they weren't taught it themselves.

So, forgive me if you are in the small, single digit percentage of teachers who already know all of this stuff, but I am now going to regurgitate what I teach students about punctuation. You may find, even if you are quite confident in this arena, that there is stuff you don't know, and, as such, I'd advise that you don't skip this bit even if you are confident. You might be surprised.

WHAT'S A PERIOD, SIR?

The bedrock of the groove in writing is found in the periods. When working with students on punctuation, I'll ask a male student what a period is: he'll rapidly let out an embarrassed snigger causing me to jump in (before it all gets too, erm, bloody) and inform them that, as well as the first thing they thought of, it is either an interval of time or something that happens during a fixed allotment of the same. In the dizzying world of punctuation, the periods do a related job: they are an indicator of timing, and the collective noun covers three marks: the full stop, the question mark and the exclamation mark! And they all have what at the bottom? They have a full stop.

The full stop

The full stop, like all punctuation marks, is merely a piece of musical notation. This notation tells the reader that they are to stop at this point and to take a pause of — so Lynne Truss says — four seconds. As to where you put it, well therein lies the problem. As we have already seen, it's like riding a bike: once you can do it, it's second nature, but if you can't, it's a mystery as to why you're the only person unable to master something reputed to be extremely easy, and which you, standing alone, in a cloud of others' competence, cannot get anywhere near understanding.

I am not able to be of much help here. The only palpable and translatable rule that I've ever heard that makes any sense is that a sentence must have a verb in it. And there is a borderline interesting theory as to why this is: if we take the 1970s primary school classification of what a verb is, and say it is a 'doing' or an 'action' word as being a reasonable facsimile version of the truth,[1] then the reason you've got to have one in a sentence is because otherwise nothing would happen and there would be no point in the sentence existing. Great for Samuel Beckett; bad for you or me. Consequently, you could put together a reasonable argument that 'plop' is a functional and grammatically correct sentence, but that 'table' isn't.

The only real traction you can get in teaching where the full stop properly goes is by explaining that the verb (the doing word) generally has a subject (who (or which) does it): Rufus (subject) belched (verb). Often there will also be an object that the verb is being done to: Rufus (subject) belched (verb) a prawn (object).

When introducing this point I'll try a silly activity with the kids, a bit of call and response, plus the following PowerPoint slide:

Subject	Verb phrase	Object
Sir	ate	a pickle.
Michael	plays with	himself.
The teacher	likes	boys.

---

1   I am aware there are people who should get out more often and who may be red faced with anger at reading this assertion.

Of course, if you were to adapt this exercise for students beneath Year 11, then you'd have to adapt the language. In the upper ages, though, the borderline scandalous responses we get when we ask them the following questions are perfectly justifiable to anyone who isn't a priggish idiot. Introduce the task, with mock seriousness, with the following script.

"You are going to get the next answer wrong. I repeat: you are going to get the next answer wrong. The answer to the next question is either 'subject', 'verb phrase' or 'object'. I repeat again: you are going to get the next answer wrong. The answer to the next question is either subject, verb phrase or object.

"Who ate a pickle?"

They gleefully pitch in.

"You did. You did, Sir. Urgh.[2] You are a nasty, dirty pig!"

Give them your smuggest of smiles and say, again, "The answer to this question is either subject, verb phrase or object. 'Sir' is not the correct answer. Who ate a pickle?"

They cotton on and answer, "The subject."

You have won. Continue.

"What did Sir do to the pickle?"

"He verb phrased it."

"The dirty pig! What did Sir eat?"

"An object!"

---

2   Actually, I don't say pickle here. I say something substantially more risqué, but I wouldn't want people to think the recent bout of sackings I've experienced were warranted.

"Bleurggh. Who plays with himself?"

"Michael."[3]

"Nope. Try again."

"The subject."

"Yes, the subject plays with himself. What does the subject do to himself?"

"He verb phrases!"

"Yes, he does. He needs mittens. What does Michael play with?"

"His object."

"Now you're getting it. Who likes boys?"

"I do!" shouts Gavin.

"The subject!" shouts everyone else simultaneously.

"What does he do to them?"

"He verb phrases them!"

"What does the teacher like?"

"Objects!"

Gavin mumbles.

You'll also get a bit of traction out of teaching them simple (no commas), compound (one comma) and complex (more than one comma) sentences. But not much. Sadly, there is a rhythmic thing with a sentence that, if you

---

3   There is usually a Michael sporting a guilty expression.

can't hear it, will have you utterly foxed. I've heard primary teachers tell me that they get some success out of reading aloud, and then seeing if the student can somehow assimilate the rhythmic element gained from the reading, after discussion, into the writing. If it works for you, then good.

The question mark

There is nothing particularly interesting about this feller; only a small piece of knowledge that some don't know and is of minor value. I will introduce it through the use of a series of questions that I humbly ask you to answer out loud:

- What's better out of an elephant and a gorilla?

- What's a mouse when it spins?

- What's an occasional table the rest of the time?[4]

- Do I want an answer to this question?

- What about this one?

- Is this question rhetorical?

- Would you do that at home?

- Do rhetorical questions have question marks?

- See what I did there?

---

4   A Thunk from Ian Gilbert. See http://www.thunks.co.uk/.

The question mark, like the full stop, is a period: a piece of musical notation that denotes a four second pause to the reader. But it also has the squiggly bit on the top, and this, like the terms *legato* or *doloroso* on a musical score, adapts the tone of the text. The squiggle is an instruction about the cadence[5] of the preceding few words: it is an instruction that, if you are reading aloud, you should go up in tone at the end of the sentence. Unless, of course, you are Antipodean? In which case, every sentence ends in a questioning cadence? Which is really irritating? Particularly, in the case of an Australian or Kiwi supply teacher who is teaching science? And who is meant to be teaching facts? And who states every such fact as if it were a question?

The exclamation mark!

Another period. It denotes a four second pause, but the tone is affected by the weird vertical line jumping up and down on top of the full stop.

It shows this emotion:

Shock or surprise!

---

5   This is the inflection of the voice as it rises or falls at the end of a sentence.

And this one:

Fear or terror!

This one too:

When I show this picture to Year 11 boys many of them make an unpleas-antly sexist comment about the emotion on display. I don't point out to them that "blowjob" is not actually an emotional state,[6] but I struggle to put on a brave face as the picture I show them is of my wife, and it is most uncomfortable having thirty young men make lewd assertions about the

---

6   Unless done expertly.

person you most love. But I struggle on ... and tell them a story about the day the picture was taken.

By way of an explanation. My wife and I are both one bare year short of being 50 years old. We love children and are fond of babies. Despite our exalted age, we are also a bit broody at the moment. We already have three children – one of whom is a year older than the young men casting aspersions as to my wife's availability and practices – and there are sound medical, fiscal and moral reasons why we will not have another child. So, we've decided to get a cat.

Because they're the same thing really. Only cats are better, because they don't ring ChildLine when you kick them (they can't hold the phone; they haven't got hands) or call you names when you ask them to pick up their clothes. Because not only do cats rarely wear clothes, they don't *usually* talk.

The picture is of my wife on the day that she went to buy the cat. It was a Saturday morning, and I was pootling around at home when I saw my mobile was ringing. I noticed that it was Jen (this is my wife's name), and picked the phone up breezily. "Hi love," I chirruped.

"Phil!" she shouted. I had to move the phone away from my ear, so stentorian was her cry.

"You're very loud, love. Are you alright?" came the rueful response.

"I know! I'm in Lewisham!"

"Well, you were meant to go to Lewisham."

"I'm in the pet shop!"

"You were meant to be in the pet shop. Are you sure you're alright?"

"Yes! I'm fine! I'm gonna tell you something, but you won't believe me!"

"I'll believe you; go on."

"I bought the cat!"

"You were meant to buy the cat."

"Yeh, but the cat can talk!"

(Deliberate pause for ironic effect)

"Don't be ridiculous. Cats can't talk."

"I knew you wouldn't believe me. Here, I'll prove it. I'll put the cat on."

And from the end of the line came a mewling voice: "I can't be on for long, mate; I haven't got hands, you see; I find it difficult holding the phone. Phil – it is Phil, isn't it? – look, I couldn't believe it myself when I first started talking! I was astonished! Particularly, when I started talking in a broad South London accent! I'm from Persia, you know! We're not meant to speak like this."

Sadly, and I'm sorry to disappoint here, none of this is actually true. Cats can't really talk. Their tongues aren't big enough. And that picture looks nothing like my wife. We're not broody. We have a house full of teenagers. If we could give them back we would. The idea of this bout of surreal gibberish was to inform you that exclamation marks are used to show shock, surprise, fear, terror and, indeed, astonishment.

They also show volume or shouting. So, the correct way of replying to the question raised in the much misunderstood behaviour management book, "Why are you shouting at us?" is, "Because I am!" Not, "BECAUSE I AM." The technique where all the words are capitalised to show volume is a scoundrel's trick used by amateurs or Year 5s (or authors playing with irony). Yes, it connotes or denotes or whatevers shouting, but it does so without any sense of there being any real writerly control. The exclamation mark to indicate volume is a far more elegant and controlled use of the tricks available to the juvenile writer.

As a plenary, what do the exclamations in the following sentences denote? "Oh, a chocolate teapot! That's as useful as a combination of the solar alarm clock(!), and a one legged man in a bum kicking contest(!)."

The first is mild surprise, as you wouldn't be fearful, or in any way terrified, of a chocolate teapot, and astonished is perhaps a little strong (though I might be overestimating your own personal tolerances to mild excitement). The second and third seem to be doing something odd: they are trying to cloak themselves, partially to hide away in shame, between the enclosing curtains of a pair of brackets. This is an odd punctuation trick that few know, and fewer still care about. An exclamation within brackets denotes a withering satirical authorial note about the language that immediately precedes it, and is often to be found in its spiritual home, the *Daily Telegraph* letters page, where it is observable in its natural context and lives in abundance.

You'll also note in the above example that it doesn't, despite the presence of the full stop at the bottom, indicate the end of a sentence. In this, it is very much the free radical of the punctuation world. You can bung him anywhere you fancy if you wish to appear as pompous and as mortally offended as a *Telegraph* reader who has just been presented with the idea that he might have to pay tax.

As regards their use: it's such a specialist and showy trick that, like swearing in a piece of creative writing, it's best only to do it once in a blue moon, and never more than twice in the same essay.

And, finally, a word on exclamations ... you only ever use three together when you are clearly taking the piss!!!

INTERVALS

These are the comma, the semicolon and the colon. The first is vital, the other two rather easier than their somewhat mythical status suggests. If you can't use the first one, though, you can't write.

Comma rule number 1

The one everyone understands and uses, as they were taught it in primary school (no matter what age they are now), is that you use a comma to separate items in lists. Tick, VG, well done, move on quickly.

If you are working with kids for whom this hasn't sunk in yet, then an enjoyable, though admittedly intellectually un-taxing, idea is to sit in a circle and construct a surreal shopping list together. First, you teach them either the move for a comma from punctuation kung fu (you reach diagonally up into the sky with your right hand as if you were to stroke the moon, only to find it is the shape of a pussycat's chin, and you cut a shape around the imaginary chin with an accompanying sound of 'Shhh'), or just teach them to put a finger click where the commas would go.

Teacher starts: "I went to the shops and I bought a series of controlling undergarments for a morbidly obese German transsexual." Everyone makes the appropriate musical or physical intervention to signify a comma,[7] then the student to the immediate left of teacher is cued in:

"I went to the shops ..."

---

7   You have to be assertive here. Only half of them will do it, and they will do it in a listless and unanimated manner. Infect the room with your own belief at this point.

Teacher intervenes. "No, you didn't. *I* went to the shops. You didn't go to the shops. It was me. You couldn't work out where they were. I just want your surreal item. Don't introduce it. Just give me the item." Student tries again.

"Banana."

At this point you enter a philosophical discussion as to whether a banana is innately surreal, and are forced, grudgingly, to accept that it is. However, be aware at this point that accepting the banana only opens the floodgates for other fruits, none of which are properly surreal.

Teacher:	OK. We'll start again. I went to the shops and I bought an innately disappointing Balinese codpiece.
Whole class:	Shhh ...
Child to the left:	Banana.
Whole class:	Shhh ...
Second child to the left:	Plum.
Whole class:	Shhh ...
Third child to the left:	Apple.

At this point you give up expecting a response from your students that is anything other than tired mimeticism, and just accept any old rubbish. The outcome we are looking for is something along the lines of a much longer version of the following: "I went to the shops and I bought my Mum, my Nan, something unpleasant and a scarf for my dog." (Of interest here, when you show the kids this as a model, is how the meaning is changed if the first comma is omitted. Have a look.)

Should we ever get anywhere near closing the circle, in terms of having the whole thirty or so students all coming in with something suitably and creatively surreal (trust teacher, it'll never happen), and all students managing to place the signal for the comma in the right place[8] (trust teacher, it'll never happen), then, when the second to last student says their surreal item, the teacher stops anyone from making the comma signal, and then cues the next student to say 'and' before saying their own final word in surreal shopping. Finally, everyone makes the punctuation kung fu signal of the full stop (a punch with the right hand into the imagined solar plexus of an imagined opponent).

The Roman Catholic approach to never, ever putting commas before 'and' came, I think, from the British idea that you don't put a comma before 'and' if it is there to affix the last item to a list. So it is, yet-a-boring-gain, the conflation of one rule with another. I say British, because the Americans seem to very much enjoy putting a comma before 'and' if it is joining the last item in the list to everything else. This is what is known as the Oxford comma: the comma before 'and', the final comma in lists and the comma of which almost no Englishman approves. The Oxford comma is also less well known as the 'serial comma', but because serials confer less elitist cache than the name of an educational institution – the predominant social function of which seems to me is to run a deliberately arcane admissions procedure that, somehow, guarantees that around half the undergraduate body come from the private sector, thereby protecting the ruling class' view of itself as intellectually superior to poorer folk, and makes uttering the word 'meritocracy' an exercise in expressing irony – this has ensured that the Oxford version has taken off, leaving the nomenclature of 'serial', despite its greater accuracy, rather unloved.

---

8   Many drop out as they find it all too embarrassing, and those who don't often put the comma signal in before they introduce the item/piece of fruit, which is ungainly and incorrect and totally defeats the purpose of the exercise. "Comma, plum."
      "No! 'Plum, comma.' Words fail me."

Whatever they are called, there is an argument for their existence, which is probably best presented with one of those silly punctuation jokes that I hope few of you reading this will have heard. Look at the difference between the following two statements:

Tracey found herself in bed with her boyfriend, a pervert and a fool.

Here, Tracey is in bed with only one person, a person who appears to have the odd mark on the debit side. We bung the Oxford comma in, and suddenly:

Tracey found herself in bed with her boyfriend, a pervert, and a fool.

Now it is Tracey who is either adventurous or immoral, depending on how you choose to view the world.

Comma rule number 2

You were taught this at primary school too, but may well have forgotten it. The rule is that you put a comma directly before you open direct speech. Its rule has become slightly confused with the role of the colon, and there is evidence that the colon is taking the place of this second comma usage in newspapers and magazines. But it's still worth knowing and it's still worth teaching, as you've got to start with a full set of rules before you can start making conscious and decisive compromises with them; before you can shift off into writing that has been tainted by progress. The model phrase I use when teaching this is: the late middle aged schoolteacher paused and said, "Get that out of his ear, boy. You'll do him a disservice."

I will repeat the phrase with a bigger comma. Here we go:

> The late middle aged schoolteacher paused and said, "Get that out of his ear, boy. You'll do him a disservice."

The sequence of the punctuation here goes: comma – open the speech marks – capital letter (often, though not always) – text – closing interval or period (often, though not always) – closing speech marks. With any sequence of information that can be memorised, my temptation is to put some moves together, so that students may have a little more fun than merely learning it by rote. It is still rote learning, but the full body immersion of attaching movement to the words may help students to memorise them. Either way, it's more entertaining than frigidly intoning a set of bare, spartan words.

The moves are (in italics): comma *(punctuation kung fu slash)* – open the speech marks *(index and middle fingers raised on left hand, left arm in the air)* – capital letter *(clap hands above head)* – text *(trace a line with the right hand which is in the shape of a fist, from the left of your waist to the right)* – closing interval or period *(punctuation kung fu for a full stop)* – closing speech marks *(index and middle fingers raised on right hand, right arm in the air)*.

You can get a whole lesson out of this technique if you are stretched on a Friday afternoon.[9], [10]

This is actually covered in my over-priced pamphlet, *Literacy through Football Skills*.[11] The reason I include this now is because the above technique is the kind of thing that makes teachers balk for several professed reasons and for one real one. The professed reasons are that my kids/I would hate to be

---

9   Message to Toby Young: this is ironic.

10   Message to teachers: the previous footnote is a lie.

11   Phil Beadle, *Literacy through Football Skills* (Carmarthen: Crown House Publishing, 2009).

taught in this manner, and that it is somehow anti-intellectual to laugh joyously when you are learning and that play and rigour are mutually exclusive. Education, over recent years, has been subject to a number of ideologically sponsored drives intended to make subject matter more challenging (broadly good up until the point it becomes merely a power mad secretary of state inflicting his own prejudices on children he doesn't understand, and the like of whom he has never met outside of a photo opportunity) and pedagogy more Dickensian (bad, of course, unless you see a career opportunity in trumpeting specious non-ideas in a short lived column on the *Telegraph* blog rubbishing any attempt to make education holistically nourishing).

Of the objection, I/my kids/the kids I teach would not like learning like this, I would answer that they would be the first children I had ever met who would choose to be bored. And of the objection about play being somehow anti-intellectual, I would reply that I am sorry your own schooling was dull, but it really isn't my fault you have chosen, out of damaged perversity, to preserve the idea that that very dullness has made you the giant you are today. Of course, learning has to be difficult sometimes. But there are more difficult and more complex things than being bored, because a government sponsored hegemony would have you believe that being disengaged is good for you.

The real one is, "I am scared it won't work, Phil." To which I'd reply, "That's OK. You're right to be scared. It probably won't work." The *Literacy through Football Skills* version of this goes as follows: comma *(drag back the ball with the right foot)* – open the speech marks *(touch the ball twice with left foot)* – capital letter *(scoop foot under the ball, looping it up into the air)* – text *(go on a mazy dribble in the direction of the goal)* – closing interval or period *(right foot on the ball)* – closing speech marks *(double touch with the right foot)*. Generally, kids take a shot at the goal after this.[12]

The reason I share this is to illustrate a process and to give you a little guidance. If you are brave enough to want to try out either dancing the second rule of comma usage, or even to try teaching it through football, then be warned: it'll fail.

The first time we did literacy through football I took my Year 11 class in a school in Croydon out onto the AstroTurf, and went through the moves, and the learning; and it bombed. I asked the boys how they thought the lesson had gone, and they replied, en masse, "Dat was worser dan your usual lessons, man." So we tried again, and again it bombed. In response to me asking how it went, Toni respectfully declaimed, "Sir, man, I respec' you an' all dat, but – out of all dat respec' I've got for you (an' all dat) – you wanna give dis up, man. Coz it jus' don't work. You've tried. We've tried. An' it's no damn good. Innit?" I liked Toni, but I thought the idea was still a good one, so we did it a third time, and it flew. The boys were brilliant; the learning was great.

We'd go back into the class and they'd say, at points, "Dat's de drag back comma innit, Sir?" and I'd see them, while writing, using their feet under the desk to remember the sequence as they were scribing bits of direct speech. And the lesson here is that innovative teaching methods, which are currently under some assault by the friends of those in power (this week), don't necessarily work the first time or even the second. You'll know if they ever will by the third time, though. If you believe the idea is strong, then have the guts to fail, follow your convictions, and see it through. If it is a good idea it might just take a few tweaks to make it work; there might be some logistical issues that just need ironing out through practice. Oh, and the people who argue

---

12 There is even a version of this scheme of work called literacy through AfL. Which is not, as you would think, Assessment for Learning; it's Aussie Rules Football. It kind of works nicely with indigenous kids in the Northern Territories.

that such techniques are anti-intellectual may well be something more than unimaginative bigots. Or, then again, they might be something less.

If we go back to my stock illustration of this:

> The late middle aged schoolteacher paused and said, "Get that out of his ear, boy. You'll do him a disservice."

I'd ask you a question: what do you notice about the relationship between the last two punctuation marks? You notice, I hope, that, paraphrasing Malcolm McLaren, "Speech marks they go round the outside, round the outside, round the outside; speech marks they go round the outside of the closing punctuation."

Here we are in the realms of stuff that everyone should know, but that doesn't seem to be taught in too many places I'm acquainted with. If you are going to write an essay which features quotes, then it seems only sensible that someone would have taught you, at some point, how you lay out these quotations within the context of the essay. And yet it seems that this is one of those nuances of the rules of writing that is seen as being of too small a relevance for too many kids (or teachers) to have been taught the rules. In teaching this with a new set of Key Stage 3 kids, I'll use a drama activity.

Seated in the drama circle of universal oneness, I'll ask the spunkiest kid in the class into the circle. (They'll be warned, quietly, that I will link arms with them at some point, and they are not to get so shocked by this that they hit me. It is important that you do this, as, otherwise, they might hit you.) Then, publicly, I'll ask them to just do whatever I do to them back at me. Giving it a bit of bad-man attitude, I'll approach them with a curled lip and a leery walk, and mouth the line, "Speech marks they go round the outside," at them as I indicate the universal signal of inverted commas – the index and middle fingers lifted on either hand – in their general direction. If properly prompted, they will then do it back at me. Repeat till the line, "round the outside of the closing punctuation",[13] at which point you link arms with the student and do a cyclical do-si-do round in circles till one of you falls over, or doesn't.

The point of this is to make it stick. Students are then paired off and asked to repeat what they have just seen. In truth it is rote learning. But it's a way of making rote learning seem somehow more appealing by covering it in some form of dazzle camouflage.

A BRIEF DIVERSION INTO SPEECH MARKS, QUOTATION MARKS AND INVERTED COMMAS

These are confusing, and I'll admit to having only recently got near achieving clarity with them. Like many people, I was formerly of the belief that these:' ' were called inverted commas, and that these:" " were called speech marks. And I had it that 'inverted commas'[14] were used for satirising, casting an ironic glance at the information between them: if you were to tell a bald feller, for instance, that he had 'nice' hair. I believed that they were also used to enclose titles, as in 'The Bald Feller', one of Seamus Heaney's lesser known early poems. What I mistakenly thought were called speech marks enclosed, or so I thought, both quotations, "My noble lord, Hamlet, thou art as bald as a shaved badger!"[15] and direct speech, "How's your barnet, Steve?"

But this is only partially true. Mr Gwynne has taught me that these: ' ' are called inverted commas, and that these:" " are also called inverted commas.

---

13 You will note that the usage at this point disobeys the rule I am mooting.

14 Or, as James Joyce had it, 'perverted commas'.

15 Phil Beadle, *Cockney 'Amlet* (unpublished).

However, these fellers: ' ' are called single inverted commas, and these: " " ...
Yes, you've guessed it, are called double inverted commas. Generally they do
the same thing, as I've outlined above: they separate into two sets of functions. On one side you've got the satire and titles, on the other you've got
the quotes and speech. But here's the shocker!!! They are interchangeable!!!

You can either have the singles doing the satire and the titles, and the doubles doing the quotes and speech, or the other way round: the doubles doing
the satire and the titles, and the singles doing the quotes and speech. It's
all a matter of what your house style is, and providing it remains cohesive,
and the same style is used all the way through, there's neither a right nor a
wrong way. If you look at *The Times* of London, they have the former house
style and the Manchester *Guardian* has the latter.[16]

Where it all gets even more confusing is when you have a quote within a
quote. In this case the enclosed quotation is marked off with singles within
doubles (or vice versa). Here are a couple of paragraphs which model the
way this works:

Whilst reading *Of Mice and Men*, I had an imaginary conversation with John
Steinbeck.

"Why did you write the book?" I asked him.

"I wanted to show what life was like for the itinerant farm workers dreaming
of living off 'the fatta the land'."

It was a weird conversation. Reading his work, *The Grapes of Wrath*, had made
me feel 'clever'. I asked, "Why did you put so much 'prettiness' in your work?"
And then read him a quote, "Both were dressed in denim trousers and in

---

16 Though my editor is of the following mind: "More usually you use one or the other con-
    sistently – for everything (except for quotes within quotes). Double quotes are standard
    practice in American-English, and single quotes are more common in British-English."

denim coats with brass buttons. Both wore black, shapeless hats and both carried tight blanket rolls slung over their shoulders."

And as a final piece of information, remember that for a quote within a quote the end punctuation goes.'" if it is a complete grammatical sentence (or."' if that is the house style).

Comma rule number 3

Here's where things can get a bit sticky, and I'll explain why I've come to such a simplistic and not entirely uncontroversial conclusion. Dear reader, I hang my head in abject intellectual shame, and admit, I am useless at properly understanding what a clause is.[17] I can read a dictionary perfectly well, but I just don't get it. I know that commas separate clauses, and I can put the commas in the right place, but I do it in a really clunky manner that no one's ever noticed or called me on. I noticed early on in my career that if I could get a kid to routinely apply a comma before the word 'but', then their writing might sprout meagre wings, and that, once we had this foundation cemented, we could stick more feathers on it. We'd introduce more words that you put a comma before, and bit by bit the student would begin to understand what a conjunction was, and that it was a joining word, and that, like a plasterer putting a lick of plaster over a crack in the wall, the comma indicated that you had joined these things called clauses. Neither student nor teacher could tell you what a clause was, but they both had a poster of all the joining words they could refer to and in front of which you put a comma; consequently, they could all use a comma correctly, and it didn't matter what a clause was. And we'd sing songs about it, and the kids

---

17 Editor's note: "Phil, are you sure you should be writing a book about literacy? It is easy. At its most basic, a clause contains a subject (whatever is being identified) and a predicate (whatever is stated about the subject), e.g. The man (subject) is weeping (predicate)."

in emerging stages would often spend a period of time when they'd put the comma after the conjunction,[18] but eventually, with practice, it'd stick.

This approach annoys purists, and it is wilfully and deliberately under-complicated but, trust me, it works. Commas before conjunctions is, for me, aside from the instruction to wear a condom, the most important thing any child will learn at school. And we don't teach them it. David Didau, whose book, *The Secret of Literacy*,[19] came out long before this extended rant – and which, sadly for me, is probably the better of the two books – once questioned me on this. His well-phrased query was, "Is this in the realms of useful, but not true?" I've had time to think about his question, and my answer is, "No, David, it is useful and, furthermore, it is true."

THE CONNECTIVES/ CONJUNCTIONS CONUNDRUM

This should go in the section on grammar being easy, but one of the reasons writers have to know a little *really very basic* grammar is that it bashes up against the rules of punctuation; and this is a case in point. In order to properly apply the most important of all the comma usages, you have, first of all, to know a little about how the joining words work.

There is a word that began to proliferate in British pedagogical discourse a decade or so ago, which is not at all properly understood by anyone other than Ros Wilson. It has become a catch-all for joining words ever since it was introduced to teachers by the National Strategies. That word is 'connective'.

---

18 They all do this at an early stage. I have no idea why. You have to mark it out of them.
19 David Didau, *The Secret of Literacy: Making the Implicit, Explicit* (Carmarthen: Independent Thinking Press, 2014).

'Connective' is basically a collective noun, which covers a variety of different types of words. We won't go too far with it in this section, but amongst the words that nestle beneath the cover-all 'connective' are conjunctions.

The conjunctions are basically the joining words, and they separate into two different varieties: coordinating and subordinating. In layman's terms, the coordinating conjunctions (e.g. and, but, or, nor, yet) add two independent clauses together to make what is called a compound sentence; the subordinating conjunctions (e.g. how, when, where, since, because) add clauses together to make a complex sentence, in which the subordinate clause (usually after the main clause) wouldn't make sense on its own.

The good news is that it doesn't matter that much which is which, as they all need a comma before them if they are the joining word in the middle of a sentence.[20]

Coordinating conjunctions

The coordinating conjunctions come with a charmingly drab, and arguably inaccurate, old school mnemonic – FANBOYS – to help you remember their names (or at least some of them). We will now re-enact that mnemonic with some illustrations of how it interfaces with commas:

He went to the shop, for he found himself to be completely empty.

He went to the shop, and found it as vacant and as desolate as his own paltry soul.

---

20 However, my editor informs me that she would generally only use a comma when the second clause can stand alone or makes sense in its own right. You are free to decide here whether the kids' examiners will know this and to act accordingly.

Neither did he go to the shop, **n**or did he go to the pub.

He went to the pub, **b**ut it didn't exist any more.

Either he will go to the shop, **o**r he will remain static.

He went to the shop, **y**et he found it didn't, in any way, allay his existential dread.

He went to the shop, **s**o five minutes of the day passed.

There's an adult rejection of this, which is: there're too many commas, Phil, too many commas! I can't cope with so many of them. They make me jittery. Relax. You may choose to leave a few out, and no one will think the worse of you. But, at what Ros Wilson calls the Emergent Stage of writing, I think it's best that students are taught a set of rules they can cling to and make reference to. Learning how to write can make you feel like you are being tossed about on a leaky boat in a tempest; it helps to have a mast.

Subordinating conjunctions

Subordinating conjunctions, which link a main clause to a subordinate clause (one that doesn't make sense on its own), generally do not have a comma before them if the main clause comes first in the sentence and the subordinate clause comes after.[21] What is interesting here, though, is that if the subordinate clause starts the sentence, then it is followed by a comma. An example:

> If I can get my trembling fingers to behave, I will wrap them round a razor blade.

Here the subordinate clause comes first. If it stood on its own, the reader would be left asking the question, "Yeh? And? Then what happened?" In the next example, where the clauses are swapped about, you are not meant to use a comma:

> I will wrap them round a razor blade, if I can get my trembling fingers to behave.

But I have put one there, as I like it like that. I will leave it to you if you are going to go with the prescriptive or the feel orientated version I recommend. If you do ask students to use commas before subordinating conjunctions, it is unlikely you will ever be told off for doing so, and it makes it all so much easier. Here is a list of them. You may wish to print them out and stick them on the wall.

---

21 But, again, we ask, "Do the examiners know this?"

after	although	as
as if	as long as	as much as
as though	because	before
even if	even though	how
if	in order that	inasmuch
lest	now that	provided (that)
since	so that	than
that	though	till
unless	until	when
whenever	where	wherever
while		

Comma rule number 4 – adverbial starts

The simplest way into adverbial starts is to use the primary school idea of the 'ly' starter (or opener): adverbs of manner. If you start a sentence with an adverb which, broadly, describes how you do something, then you put a comma after it. In their simplest terms, loads of adverbs end in 'ly': silently, cleverly, sophisticatedly. Though not all words that end in 'ly' are adverbs. The best way to check whether an 'ly' word is an adverb is to see if you can put the word after 'pooh' and use it as an instruction. If it reads like a surreally plausible thing to do, then it is an adverb; if it reads like a one-and-a-half-year-old describing what they have just done, then it isn't.

- Pooh cleverly – plausible, though surreal; therefore, it's an adverb.

- Pooh ugly – a one-and-a-half-year-old's accusation.

- Pooh sophisticatedly – happens at the Queen's house; therefore, it's an adverb.

- Pooh lovely – maybe in certain latitudes, but not here.

- Pooh disappointingly – it's your age, dear; it's an adverb.

Clearly, the simplest version of the adverbial start (or fronted adverbial for poshos) is the 'ly' opener. What the comma does here is that it gives the sentence a little James Bond wink, rhythmically. Read aloud these two versions of the same sentence:

Silently he farted.

Silently, he farted.

The first is bald and matter of fact; the second, if you click your fingers on the comma, is slyer, more cocksure, more at ease with manipulating the rhythmic patterns of speech and the emotions of ladies.

The issue for students and teachers is that not all adverbs end in 'ly'. There's a whole raft of them that go by the name of conjunctive adverbs (or conjuncts). In alphabetical order, and in photocopiable form, these are:

additionally	also	alternatively
although	besides	consequently
furthermore	hence	however
incidentally	indeed	instead
likewise	meanwhile	moreover
nevertheless	next	nonetheless
otherwise	plus	rather
similarly	since	so
still	then	therefore
thus	whereas	

If you start a sentence with any of these, you put a comma immediately after them.

However, there's a matter of style here: you might find that it's better not to start the sentence with a conjunctive adverb and just tack the clause onto the previous clause; in which case you would use a semicolon. But we'll get on to that a bit later.[22]

Often, adverbials come within a sequence of words that might be termed clauses or phrases. Like straight adverbs of manner, they give additional information about what's going on, and they separate down into adverbials of:

- Time: While Sir was calling the register, Jason kicked Kevin.

---

22 There is an important piece of information about these that you might want to look at now if you can stand the boredom. It is in the grammar section in the bit about adverbs on page 181.

- Place: In my classroom, it is cramped, and it is vile, and it is wet.

- Manner: As if he owns the place, he's strutting the corridors.

- Degree: As clever as you think you are, you are not.

- Condition: If I can be arsed, I'll mark your book.

- Concession: Although he was in the top set, Arthur was surprisingly stupid.

- Reason: Because the head teacher was slurring, assembly was cancelled.

- Purpose: So he could replenish the supply in his 'water' bottle, the head teacher visited the Russian off-licence.

Note that these all start with conjunctions (joining words), which rather disproves the antiquated idea that you should not start a sentence with one, and that they (mostly) have a comma after the phrase. They also go by the name of subordinate clauses, in that they are not the main piece of information in the sentence, and you usually mark subordinate clauses off from the main clause with a comma.

Comma rule number 5 – to mark off embedded clauses

This is the trick that separates the A* writers from the merely functionally literate: where an additional piece of information has been inserted into a sentence that would make perfect sense without this information, you mark off the diversion with a pair of commas on either side of it. This can be difficult to teach, but my way of doing so has always been to use a football analogy. Just as a football player approaching an opponent has a destination, so sentences too have a place they want to get to: the full stop. The writer intends the sentence to make a cohesive point before he gets to it. As such, we might regard a simple sentence as an 'A to B sentence':

A   B

Paul Gascoigne tripped over the ball.

An embedded clause is where it continues from A to B, but takes a detour via C:

A   C   B

Paul Gascoigne, being both fat and drunk, tripped over the ball.

Here, the information that Gazza had enjoyed a shandy and a kebab is the new information and, being the embedded clause,[23] it is marked off with commas.

This, however, isn't all: it leads us on to the uber-nerdy issue with single embedded conjunctive adverbs being used in the middle of a sentence for effect. See the first sentence of this paragraph for how this works. It's a fairly bog standard writerly trick (my friend and guru, Ros Wilson, describes it as "the two comma trick"), and I wouldn't take too much pride in being able to do it if you are an adult. It is, nevertheless, a useful show-off in Key Stage 4. And you might find, moreover, that students enjoy being able to do it.

---

23 Note in this sentence how embedded clauses link up with commas before conjunctions. Ordinarily, one might expect there to be a comma before the 'and' but, much like in this sentence, the fifth comma use trumps the third and the embedded clause cancels out the need for the comma before the conjunction.

BRACKETS AND DASHES

The reason this sits directly after the bit on embedded clauses is that both brackets and dashes perform a similar function to these particular commas: the sentence could cope and would read perfectly well without the information they enclose, but there is a piece of additional information you feel necessary – for whatever reason – to lodge in the middle of the sentence (or occasionally, in the case of brackets, at the end).

If we rapidly sketch through the rules, you use brackets to:

1. Enclose parenthetical (additional) information within a passage

This is by far the main usage of the bracket (this section is a bit boring, isn't it?) and is the one that students need to be fluid with. It is an unpleasant surprise (to me) that students are rarely as capable with these as they should be and, whilst too many brackets all over a text looks either a bit showy (or that you are subject to a certain intellectual skittishness), not using them at all means you are playing without a part of the kit, and there are certain effects that you will not be able to achieve.

Then we get on to the closing bracket's relationship with the full stop. Punctuation outside of a pair of brackets is decided by the structure of the main sentence. When a sentence ends with a parenthesis, we need to know whether the parenthesis forms part or all of the sentence. If it is a complete grammatical sentence then the stop goes inside; if it is only part of the sentence then the stop goes outside.

2. Insert comments or information into direct quotations

I'm going to quote from *Macbeth* here to exemplify this, as Shakespeare's lawyers are a bit sleepy:

Is this a dagger which I see before me, [Nope.]

The handle toward my hand? Come, let me clutch thee. [He is actually talking to an imaginary dagger here: woo woo.]

I have thee not, and yet I see thee still.

Art thou not, fatal vision, sensible

To feeling as to sight? Or art thou but

A dagger of the mind [possible reasons for the dagger to be there: (1) the witches put it there, (2) the plot: she gone, (3) magic mushrooms], a false creation?

3. Identify errors in text, by use of the word [sic] within brackets

This is when you are quoting something in which there is an error, a piss-smelling [*sic*], a moonerspism [*sic*] or something of that elk [*sic*].

You will also note that, just to complicate things even further, square brackets were used in the previous two examples. This is because they are editorial additions.

Which of the three usages above did you already know? The first one. Which of them do you think your students should be using in a show-offy manner in exams? Why, all of them Mr Teacher. One of the keys with punctuation is playing with it, using it to the point that it becomes an intrinsic part of the creativity of your writing. And it helps if you are able to use a full range, throwing in the odd plausibly esoteric effect that is one of the minor uses, like the two subsidiary rules for bracketing above. It shows the examiner that you are such a master of writing that even the minor effects obey you.

Dashes are in the realm of something that you were taught at school but did not help you: you use a dash to attach additional or ancillary information. When you were at primary school, and you were coming to the end of a line, and still the word wasn't finished, your version of Sister Dimpnah would advise that you use a dash at the end of a line (where the first word hung unfinished, unsatisfied and incomplete – that is, a soft return), and then put the rest of the word on the next line, perhaps prefixed with a dash. In a way, the teacher had accidentally hit on a universal and profound truth, but had only chanced on it by ignorance and never went any further with it. The transcendental piece of information her advice had hinted at is the following (and excuse the primary school capitalisation here): DASHES COME IN TWOS. You can use a dash on its own, as it can also perform the same function as a colon, BUT THEY MOSTLY COME IN TWOS. CAN YOU HEAR ME AT THE BACK? DASHES COME IN TWOS.

Your teachers confused dashes with hyphens, which join two words together to make one word, and it is an easy mistake to make, because, after all, they look almost exactly the same. But they are not the same. The hyphen (-) is a solitary animal, but he is a match-maker, seeking to form relationships between words that would otherwise have stayed single. Pairs of dashes are in an unhappy marriage. They come together,[24] but are always apart. The dash (–) is used to set off additional material within a sentence, often in order to emphasise it. A DASH IS NOT A HYPHEN! Sometimes they get confused. A hyphen generally joins words or parts of words to indicate a connection; a dash does not.[25]

What dashes do is pretty well the same as the first use of the bracket, but whilst the bracket indicates that the information contained within it is subordinate to the rest of the sentence, pairs of dashes emphasise that information as being important. It doesn't matter if you find the nuances of this difficult to master, as basically no one can. But there is a social class element here: if you glance at *The Times*, you'll note that the columnists they employ rarely bother with the humble bracket, as it is very much the kind of skill a student from an inner city comp might be expected to be able to use. Their technique seems to be to replace brackets, which are felt rather down at heel through overuse, with the rather more showy, rather more pristine pair of dashes.

Same rules apply though. The sentence must be able to continue in a perfectly orderly fashion if the gear bracketed within the dashes – or dashed within the brackets – did not exist. Teaching this technique and getting students to apply it – initially experimentally – does give their writing the see-through veneer of sophistication.

Here are some examples:

• Three herberts – Herbert, Herbert and Herbert – bunked off my lesson.

---

24 I think I may have inadvertently hit upon the secret to a happy marriage here.
25 It's worth knowing that when typing a dash, you need to use an en rule (which is the length of a printed *N*) with a space on either side of it, or an em rule (the length of a printed *M*) which can be used closed up to the text before and after it.

- What he feels for that woman – he is madly in love with her – is permanent.

- Learning to write – the process of encoding meaning – isn't easy.

How would you punctuate the following examples, remembering to use dashes in pairs (to shout) or brackets (to understate)?

1   Miss Pringle being an outrageously excellent teacher wanted the best for her students.

2   There was something about the bloke teaching us punctuation he's going bald, bald I tell you that we didn't like.

3   Arsenal under the auspices of Arsène Wenger clearly a mid-table outfit will finish below QPR in the premiership this year.[26]

COLONS AND SEMICOLONS

The colon is easy: it indicates that what comes after it is an illustration or a clarification of what comes before it. I teach my students that it stands for a phrase: "Let me tell you about it." The colon is easy – let me tell you about it – it indicates that what comes after it is an illustration or clarification of what came before.

Often, because I am mad, I will bring in two tennis balls to illustrate the rhythmic thing it does when you are reading: it gives just about the same amount of white space in the diatribe as the gap between a tennis player throwing the balls up into the air and then hitting them. In class, I will

---

26   I wrote this worksheet in a bout of the most ridiculous optimism. QPR were relegated at the end of the year; Arsenal finished fourth, as usual.

demonstrate this effect by reading a few sentences featuring a colon and throwing both balls in the air at the point the colon appears. As they go up into the air, they actually look like a colon. You can see here on what paltry grounds legendary status is awarded. The only other thing that teachers need to know about the colon is that it is the one that introduces a list. If you introduce lists with a semicolon, then you are wrong to do so.

It is the semicolon that causes all the heartache and all the worry. It shouldn't. The rules are not *that* difficult. But ...

One of the lovely people I list in the acknowledgements is my friend, Mr James Stafford. I use 'Mr' here as a mark of respect, as we share a code orientated around having proper manners that few would understand. Mr Stafford and I worked together in a tough school in Croydon, in which we were both perceived as being a little too fissile by management. He is the co-inventor of teacher top trumps, a former doorman at One Nation, a graduate of Oxford University and the most intelligent man I have ever had the pleasure of knowing. Mr Stafford and I have sat in bars in lower Croydon, Littlehampton and Camden and discussed the semicolon at length – our wives no longer attend, of course – and have concluded that if one is to have any long term relationship with writing, then it will necessarily also involve a relationship with the semicolon and, because she is mercurial, it will be a relationship in which you are never really the dominant partner. The semicolon is more an art than a science. But that doesn't mean you should give up on it.

If we examine the weight of writing experience of one of those two fellers in the pub and the academic excellence of the other, then we can draw some conclusions: neither the Oxford English graduate nor the former broadsheet education columnist really have the first clue of how to master the semicolon, and both of us overuse them. What might this suggest about the second year professional who is marking your students' papers? Yes, that's right. They don't necessarily know where they go either. Of interest here is the fact that exam boards have previously given out guidance to markers that they are to give credit for effort in terms of trying to use this particular punctuation mark; and also that the independent sector in Europe tends to regard a semicolon in an essay as the surest sign of plagiarism there is(!). Before we have a look at where they go, I'll hand you a hot tip that has always worked for me, which is a little unethical (but works): when working with young people on English controlled assessments, I will give them the guidance that (if they can't understand where to place the semicolon) they just change three commas over the piece into semicolons. No one has ever noticed or called me on this.

For those interested in at least trying to get things as right as they can, the rules are as follows:

1   It shows that there is a relationship between two erstwhile independent clauses. And that relationship can be oppositional.

2   It is used for when there are lists within lists to mark off the top lists.

3   It follows a conjunctive adverb in the middle of a sentence.[27]

The second one can appear quite high order, but basically it's where there are top lists and sub-lists within those top lists. The example below is this usage at its most simple. (It can get a lot more complicated than this, but the example shows the principle well enough.)

One of my mates lives in Littlehampton, Sussex; one lives in Beckenham, Kent; and one lives in Tokyo, Japan.

Without the semicolons separating the top lists it would be a little like a comma car crash.

---

27   There is more on conjunctive adverbs in the section on adverbs on pages 181–182.

The first one is where the big marks are kept: it's basically where you've got two clauses and you suspect they would fit together nicely in some form of syntactical marriage. And the benefits to students, in terms of how their work is seen – remember, most people regard the semicolon as almost completely impenetrable – come in the form of extra marks that go towards better versions of the certificates they will eventually be awarded. This is best illustrated with reference to one of my favourite uses of semicolons this year: Simon Jenkins' first sentence in an article about lobbying in *The Guardian* included the perfectly punctuated phrases, "I chat; you lobby; he is corrupt."[28] They are three clauses and could quite reasonably have been separate sentences, but the semicolons display an awareness of rhythm and of there being an audience for the work; they deliberately manipulate the scansion of the sentence, just as I have done in this sentence. So, in terms of kids using them, they are more likely to go in the place of full stops than they are commas, since they join independent clauses together, and independent clauses can be sentences.

Ultimately though, it *is* more an art than a science, and students should be encouraged to play with them and get them wrong. There may well be an array of incorrectly applied semicolons throughout this book; you won't have noticed them; I have been playing with semicolons and getting them wrong for decades; often I'll throw them in – deliberately – for rhythmic effect.

---

28 Simon Jenkins, 'Cameron Has Failed to Resist the Lunchtime Lobbyists' Lure', *The Guardian* (19 July 2014). Available at: http://www.theguardian.com/commentisfree/2013/jul/18/lobbying-buying-influence-taints-politics/.

APOSTROPHES

The only real contribution I've made to British pedagogy is through the simple technique of combining rote with movement. It's not much (either in size or in intellectual weight). And we start off the bit about apostrophes with one of these: when first introducing the subject with pupils, I will recite a little speech and do some movements, asking the students to copy them.

"There are two"	Raise index and middle fingers on right hand into the sky. Which way round you have these is up to you. One of the two varieties is held to be rude.
"Uses of the apostrophe"	Still in the air, wiggle the index finger of your right hand.
"One"	Middle finger on the same hand in the air. Again, be certain you know which way round you want this finger as it can cause offence.
"Possession"	Clutch both hands to your heart.
"Two"	Two fingers to the world again. Then start making a scissors action.
"Contraction"	Mime rather too glib a circumcision.[29]

---

29 If working in primary or Key Stage 2, don't do this. It works if you just use your hands to show something getting smaller by bringing them together.

The contractive apostrophe causes few problems in British schools: this is where the apostrophe is used to show a letter has been missed out. The only issues are when students do'nt [*sic*] properly understand it and put the apostrophe where they have guessed it should go, rather than where a letter has been missed out.

The real issue is with its brother, the possessive apostrophe; and that issue is substantial. My unevidenced guess would be that in the region of 50 per cent of the people reading this book don't know how to use them. As a consequence, outside of the top set in a decent school, we are totally awash with crap apostrophes, as kids tend towards the strategy of just putting one on the end of every word that ends in an 's'. The problem is caused, in part, by the nomenclature. It isn't really there to show possession, though it does; it is to show whether the subject of the sentence is singular or plural. If we take a student's intention after school to go to her teachers [*sic*] houses and do something terrible, because the possessive has an 's' at the end, and so does a plural, we can't tell which of these is being denoted. It might be that she is going to a few houses that belong to a series of teachers or, alternatively, more than one house owned by the same teacher who made some very good investment decisions in the late 1990s. And that is what the possessive apostrophe is for: to indicate the relative wealth of teachers.

Again, this works best by rote: "Before the 's' singular, after the 's' plural." REPEAT!

So, if the errant student is going to her teacher's houses to do something disagreeable, then we can conclude by inference and deduction that the teacher in question is singular, and, along with the teacher's pension, he/she should have a very comfortable retirement indeed. If, however, she was going to commit a nuisance at her teachers' houses, we can conclude that it is not just a piece of vindictive behaviour about one teacher, and that she is a very naughty student indeed. The possessive apostrophe here will not tell you how many teachers she is abusing, just that it is more than one. When a personal name ends with s, the greatest consistency can be achieved by throwing out any exceptions and treating them with the full apostrophe 's', so James's and Camus's (or alternatively, the apostrophe only, so James' and Camus').

Things get further confused with exceptions:

- There's no possessive apostrophe on its. "'I' 'T' APOSTROPHE 'S' can only ever mean it is." REPEAT!

- Neither is there one on his, hers or theirs.

In terms of how to teach this, after the initial information has been drummed in we go out on a walk, with cameras, and create a display of all the crap apostrophes we can find in our local area. We put these up on the wall with commentary written by the kids as to why the apostrophe is wrong and what an idiot the person is who made this sign.

My favourite of these is of a pub that no longer exists which was called, according to the sign, The Two Halve's. This was one student's commentary on the sign, "For God's sake! In how many different ways can one sign be wrong? First, you cannot have a possessive apostrophe when there is nothing to possess. The halves don't possess anything. So it must be a contractive apostrophe, but that would mean the sign said, 'The Two Halve is', which is wrong again in so many ways. And, finally, why not just call it The Pint?"

TEACHERS NOT BEING MODELS OF STANDARD ENGLISH

DA KING AND I

I'm going to approach this by way of my favourite story about a student, ever. Sadly, I am now of the advanced age that I can mumble the following phrase without irony, and that phrase is: some of my best friends are head teachers. In 2010/2011, the school I worked at in Wandsworth was run by my mucker, Rob. Rob, being a mate and a former colleague from a seriously bloody tough school, was not inclined to stand for any of what he oh-so-charmingly termed my "prima donna nonsense", and on my first day presented the antidote to such behaviour by being entirely unpleasant: "This nonsense about not having a form class stops from this moment. Furthermore, you are doing break duty and a lunch duty – SMT money means SMT responsibilities – and here's your bottom set Year 10s. Enjoy. Ho, ho, bloody ho!"

My Year 10s, known somewhat euphemistically as 'the nurture group' by the rest of the teachers, were basically a plethora of the kind of Dickensian characters you get in the bottom set of a sink school in a deprived area of London: the boy who ate only crisps, whose trousers regularly split and whose thighs emitted polyester sparks as he waddled while attempting to play football; the Spanish boy who all the girls fancied, and who, in his proud and abject idiocy, confirmed that all the girls were also idiots; the boy who had recently returned from boarding school in Nigeria and bore the scars, and whom I wished I was able to cuddle and tell him it would be OK, but it probably wouldn't be. And, finally, the young man whom we shall refer to with his own chosen nomenclature: Da King!

Da King and I started brightly enough, playing together with notions of teacher authority. But our relationship went a little downhill when it transpired dat Da King did not believe in punctuality. He would arrive to lessons a statutory eight minutes late, and would announce his arrival by pushing the classroom door open with a flourish, entering hands aloft, strutting, receiving an imagined ovation and proclaiming, "Yes peepul! Da King has arrived!"

(To which I might occasionally respond by half muttering, "Morning Princess. You're eight minutes late.")

On his birthday, Da King's Mum had given him a belt buckle that took the shape of a large dollar sign. And it revolved! As it was Da King's special day, he arrived this time a statutory twelve minutes late, flung the door open with his ordinary flourish, only this time stopping dramatically to revolve the buckle, which span as impressively and as long lastingly as a gin hangover, before proclaiming proudly, "Bling, Beadleman. Be jealous. Berrrrling!!!" And still the buckle turned, undermined only marginally by the fact that it was obviously cheap painted plastic.

Over the space of our year together I learned much from Da King. He learned precisely nothing from me. He was, however, responsible for perhaps the greatest single thing any student has ever said to me.

Because the English curriculum has historically been written by academics/goons, you do not actually have to read a single book to be certified in

GCSE English.[1] As a result, Da King had not read a single book since he had left the warm bosom of his former primary school. We find ourselves reading in class, Sir leading a small group, and the focus is causing him actual physical pain. There is a saying in the inner cities that, if you believe something to be the embodiment of lacerating boredom and all-encompassing ennui, you describe it as being "a long ting". At the end of the reading Da King, who had held it together remarkably well for the five minutes or so he was required to concentrate on something of intellectual validity or consequence, gave voice to a feeling that had clearly been troubling him for the whole extended period.

"Oh Christ, Sir, Beadleman!!! Dat was a LONG, LONG, LONG, LONG TING!"

I pointed out to Da King dat da genre we were reading was called 'the short story', and that, actually, some people like to read for fun.

And he was offended by the idea. "No way! NO WAY! People read for fun??? Sir man, Beadleman ... doze people are dumb!"

Da King was of the belief that one of the key means of transmission of knowledge – reading – was something dat only really stoopid people do. As a result of this, his language was rarely as well ordered and as fluent as it might have been. I once witnessed a conversation between Da King and his oppo, Junior, during my much detested lunch duty, that went a little like this:

Da King: Innit?

Junior: Innit doh?

Da King: Innit?

---

1   "Some mistake there, surely?" "No. No mistake, Mr Beadle. There is nothing to see here. Move on."

Junior:	Innit doh?
Da King:	Innit?
Junior:	Innit doh?
Da King:	Innit?
Junior:	Innit doh?
Da King:	Innit?
Junior:	Innit doh?
Da King:	Innit?
Junior:	Innit doh?
Da King:	Innit?
Junior:	Innit doh?
Da King:	Innit?
Junior:	Innit doh?
Da King:	Innit?
Junior:	Innit doh?

Forty-five minutes and not a single other bloody word.

And here we come to the denouement of Da King's story. We had an up and down relationship, as I wasn't as good with him as I am reputed to be; despite my best efforts and reputation, I failed him, every day. One day, when he was in a really good mood in a computer room, he turned to Junior, and because he was in a super good mood, said, "Innit? Beadleman, dat you is, erm ... y'know ... safe!" In inner city London "safe" is the ultimate teacher accolade, and certainly Da King was not always of the mind dat I was safe, and so I was pleased to enjoy the brief break in hostilities. But he wanted to go further, as he hadn't quite expressed the love and respec' he felt (albeit fleetingly). "Innit doh dat you is … innit dat you is … wha'a'mean is … innit dat you is …" And you could see his expression becoming increasingly pained as he searched his mind for another positive piece of language, only to find it was absent. He didn't cry. Nor did I. Externally.

In the end, he came up with quite an elegant solution: as he didn't have any more material, he changed the media and styled it out by singing. "Innit tho dat you is safe," he sang really quite sweetly, adding little wicka, wicka wickas whilst miming the action of scratching a record.

Had Da King wanted to say something unpleasant and derogatory, he had a whole arsenal of putrid insults readily available. But, like many of his fellow passengers in the nurture group, he did not have the words to be nice.

What is odd here is that Da King's mother is an articulate and impassioned woman. But she is a single mother and has to hold down three jobs in order to keep a roof over her head, and Da King is babysat every night by a screen on which he plays *FIFA Soccer* all the time. And I mean 'all the time' to have a literal thud here. He does not do anything else outside of school. He has no present role model of how to communicate effectively with human beings.

ALL TEACHERS TO USE STANDARD ENGLISH AS THE ONLY LANGUAGE FOR INSTRUCTION AND TO INSIST THAT STUDENTS USE IT TOO

This is why the teacher must speak in Standard English: because he or she may be the only real role model for how to speak this language that the young person has. Furthermore, the teacher must also insist that the only language to be used in the classroom by the students is Standard English. If they do not have access to and practise with this language then they are doomed.

I am alive to the irony here of transcribing the way in which I allowed Da King to talk in my classroom, which is multi-ethnic London slang. I have made up for this recently, and indeed did so with a different class in the same school. I tried with the nurture group, but their issues were so deeply entrenched they could not be solved by one part-time English teacher over the space of a bare year. With the other class, the insistence that they were to leave their dialect form at the door paid substantial dividends. Initially, it felt like they were imitating posh people, but slowly the habits became entrenched. Their results were outstanding (86% A–C in English in a former special measures school, and the highest CVA in inner London). This approach, when combined with other rigours, made a tangible contribution to the results in the school where I worked, which was the most improved school in the country in 2011/2012.

There is an uncomfortable sense here for those of us who entered the teaching profession in possession of an idea of ourselves as owning a certain left wing radicalism; we who regard a person's dialect as a vital part of their identity and seek to protect working class children's rights to view their own language positively. By way of explanation, I too am in possession of a dialect form that I love and am proud of.

My old man and I often frequent the rub-a-dub of a Sunday lunchtime. I'll get the sherberts in these days as Dad's a bit boracic since he retired. Whilst at the bar, the barman will ask me, "What jam jar's your old man driving nowadays? 'E done well for 'imself, di'n't 'e?"

Sitting down, with a pair of foaming Nelsons,[1] I'll ask him, "How's your Emmas, Dad?"

"What? Me Clements?"

"Yeh. How's your Rockfords?"

"Me Judiths?"

"Your farmers?"

"Me Chalfonts?"

"Yep. How's your Norberts?"

"What me four minute miles? They're a proper Michael Caine. Me Khyber's in a right two and eight."

---

1   Nelsons – Nelson Mandelas – pints of Stella.

SOLUTION 2: ALL TEACHERS TO USE STANDARD ENGLISH
AS THE ONLY LANGUAGE FOR INSTRUCTION

In Cockney rhyming slang we have at least fifteen separate synonyms for haemorrhoids.[2] The Eskimos? They have many different words for snow. In working class London, we too have a proud specialism ... The point here is that we all have dialect forms that we are proud of, but, if you want to improve your students' ability to write, it is better if neither you nor they use them in the classroom. Check 'em in with your coat as you enter the door. This action is more urgent in some communities than others. In London we have the issue of having countless young people, like Da King, who are not able to speak in any other language than multi-ethnic London slang, and for whom every single sentence they ever speak ends in 'innit'. In Newcastle, people are rightly proud of their linguistic heritage, but these oral forms and declensions slip into their writing. Similarly in Yorkshire where 'nowt' and 'owt' creep into essays.

For instance, the way a working class Londoner conjugates the past tense version of the verb 'to be' when it is in the negative is:

I weren't.

You wasn't.

He/she/it wasn't.

We wasn't.

You wasn't.

They wasn't.

---

2   Emmas, Clements, Sigmunds, Rockfords, Chalfonts, Topps, Bernards, Plymouths, Nuremburgs, Metrics, Nobbys (or Norberts), Belindas, four minutes, Sieg Heils. These include the seemingly impenetrable Judiths (Judith Chalmers – farmers – Farmer Giles – piles).

This leads students, when asked what Lennie and George were doing in the bunkhouse, to conclude that "They wasn't doing nothing."

I have previously expressed a scepticism about correcting the spoken language of a student, and I think in *How to Teach* I said that no one has a right to tell anyone else that how they speak is wrong. I haven't entirely changed my mind, but I think it is possible to teach students the skills of expressing themselves orally in functional Standard English without inadvertently passing on the message that their own cultural form is somehow incorrect.

ROZZIE WILSON SAYS

Ros Wilson, the originator of Big Writing that is used in many/most/all primary schools, does not drink gin from pewter flagons, as I may have led some attenders of my training sessions to believe. She does, however, repeat the following phrase in flat Northern vowels while in a variety of well-appointed hotel bars late at night with the writer of this book, "If you can't speak it. You can't write it. Why does nobody know this, Phil?"

If you think about writing you might find reason to describe it as being nothing more than thought transcribed. You might further conclude that most thought comes in the form of suppressed spoken language, and that the more able you are to articulate thought in speech, the more able you will be with the written word. In the process of writing this book, I am merely typing words that come into my head that I am deliberately not saying out loud as, even though I am secluded in my study, they would place me perilously close to having to view myself as (I am told) others see me.

So, if we want to improve students' ability to write, we would do well to first improve their ability to express themselves in the spoken word. We should also do so because being able to speak well and being able to articulate their internal world is of immense value in itself: it will make our students more successful; it will make them better friends; it will make them more interesting, more attractive, more charming; it will make them more able to understand the world, more able to articulate nuance, and less likely to hit things.

One of the means Ros uses to get better quality talk from the little people she works with is through a concept of hers called "up-skilling talk". Ros routinely asks students to discuss what they are going to do in their upcoming piece of writing before they ever get to sit, pen in hand; but she instructs them to "talk it in posh". Now, you might have a class based objection to this particular piece of language, and might want to refer to it, as Ruth Miskin does, as their "book voice", or as I do when this process is relocated to secondary schools, in "GCSE English"; but the results are extraordinary. When asked to talk it in posh, young people's accents change, which, of course, is repulsive; but so, too, does their language. To give you an insight into how this works, I'm going to ask you to go through the lyrics from an old music hall number and talk it in posh (by which I don't just mean the accent; speak the words posh people would use). See what happens.

The lyrics can be found here http://lyrics.wikia.com/Traditional:Show_Me_The_Way_To_Go_Home

What do you notice? Your language has gone up several NCAT levels. Now transcribe this and you've got sophisticated written expression.

The real second verse of this goes:

> Indicate the way to my habitual abode
>
> I'm fatigued and I wish to retire
>
> I had an alcoholic beverage 60 minutes ago
>
> And it went straight to my cerebellum.
>
> Where ever I may perambulate along
>
> On land or sea or atmospheric vapour
>
> You can always hear me harmonising this melody
>
> Indicate the way to my habitual abode.

However, there is an interesting alternative take on this from blogger and teacher Andrew Old, which in the interest of getting things as right as possible, is worth looking at.

> I think I've challenged the idea that practising speaking is *necessarily* practising writing. The main objection is that if a child can already speak far better than they can write, then no amount of improvement in speaking will help, but also we do often write better than we speak simply because we have longer to think about the words. I can't imagine it would never be a good idea to work on spoken language, but the general rule of thumb is that what you practise is what you learn, rather than practising one skill and have it immediately transfer into another. On the other hand, I'm sure there are plenty of skills where verbal practice is very useful and plenty of students with much to gain (EAL being an obvious example). Even in maths, verbal work is useful for mental calculations. I think I

challenged a situation where somebody implied that encouraging students to speak would always be good for their writing, rather than one where the speaking had a specific purpose, i.e. practising a specific skill which might then be useful.[3]

Which, as ever, is well-expressed and far more sensible than Mr Old is sometimes given credit for by people from my side of the argument. If we are to take this on board then the idea is that: when students talk about their writing, they must first imagine it as a narrative and rehearse it through speech, perhaps with a talk partner questioning them as to glitches or argumental fallacies in their expression.

This leads us towards an examination of the relationships between the various literacies and to conclude that there is a further problem with literacy in the English speaking classroom.

---

3   Old Andrew, private correspondence with author.

ORACY NOT BEING TAKEN SERIOUSLY ENOUGH, AND THE RELATIONSHIPS BETWEEN THE VERSIONS OF LITERACY NOT BEING PROPERLY UNDERSTOOD

If Ros Wilson is right, and you can't write what you can't speak, then the way in which we currently rate the three subsets of literacy needs a look. The way we currently view them is:

Reading – A fundamental and vastly important skill.

Writing – A fundamental and vastly important skill.

Oracy – A doss(y) lesson that generates no marking.

There's also the fact that the way various orthodoxies view the relationships between the three forms is actually factually incorrect. I first came across this when working on the Channel 4 adult literacy programme. At the time of the recording, adults who were scratching at the very earliest stages of being literate were assessed on reading, writing, and speaking and listening, and were taught discrete units on these key skills.[1] The people who were taught this would include the brave cab driver who never learned to read at school, but has had the guts and chutzpah to try to do something about it in adulthood. His issue is he cannot read, therefore he cannot write; but it is the reading that he wants fixed.

Instead of focusing on what he needed, however, the teaching materials and curriculum wasted his time on pointless speaking and listening activities from which he learned nothing and which completely wasted his bravery and his energy. He was forced to do this, against his will, by the people he trusted as experts to divest him of his stigma, because of the fundamental flaw in logic of the adult literacy world, which, in direct opposition to the truth, insisted that improved speaking and listening will help him to read. It's nonsense, of course. He speaks well already, and being able to speak in a more formal manner does not help you to crack the phonic code (which is what he wanted). It doesn't matter how much government institutions insist that it does, because it doesn't.

So, speaking better doesn't help you to read at the early stages. It may help you when you first encounter vocabulary when reading that you've already assimilated into your schema through aural encounters, but it does not help you to crack the code.

This issue is merely symptomatic, however, of the issues caused by teachers or commentators who conflate, and promote the conflation of, the distinct skills of reading and writing. I have lost count of the number of times some old children's laureate or other has given advice to young people that, if they want to be better writers, then they should read more. You've heard this too. You've given this advice out as well. Of course, being able to write at all is contingent on having acquired the ability to read, but really this advice is

---

1   Until they were assessed at level 1 (which contributed to government figures), at which point the writing component stopped. "Some mistake here, surely, Mr Government?" "Nothing to see here, Mr Beadle. Comb your hair."

palpable gibberish. If you want to be a better writer, then write more. Practice at one skill will not improve another distinct skill. And yes, you are right, it is more complicated than that. But not much. This attitude is a hangover from the approach to teaching kids to read that left many of my generation illiterate: the ludicrous assumption (generally put about by someone with a lot of links to publishers) that if you sit a kid down with a load of books they'll learn to read by osmosis. You do not learn by osmosis. You learn by being taught or by practising on your own. If you want young people to be better at writing, then teach them how to write. If you want young people to live enriching intellectual lives, then get them to read more.

If we refer back to the assessment of the three varieties of literacy, a certain reframing needs to take place. They should be viewed as follows:

Oracy – *The* most fundamental and most important skill.

Reading – A fundamental and vastly important skill.

Writing – A fundamental and vastly important skill.

Think about how often you spend on the first in comparison to the other two. Yes, you are a teacher and you do a lot of reading. You are probably even one of doze dumb peepul who do it for pleasure. I'd bet a bundle, though, that you spend more time communicating through speech.

Being able to articulate your thoughts adequately or better through speech is (empathy aside) the most important skill humans have to acquire; and in British schools it is a skill that has been relegated out of its natural place, so that it is perceived by a system that has been organised up to the day I am writing this[2] by one individual's bigotries and lack of cultural experience as being less important than sitting still, listening for hours and nodding deferentially at your betters. Being able to organise and articulate your thoughts

---

2   This was written on the very day Gove was sacked.

orally – be it to argue, to persuade, to describe, to inform, to entertain, even to enrapture – is pivotal to success in life. If we take the now former secretary of state[3] as an exemplar[4] here, much of his success in de-modernising British education came as a result of his undoubted eloquence. This, as evidence of high intelligence, made people frightened of arguing with him; as arguing with a loquacious man who enjoys constructing a convincing argument that black is, in fact, white is a challenging experience.

And here we arrive at the defining problem. The conclusion I have come to originates from some experience and from seeing ten times more schools in a half-term than an Ofsted inspector sees in a year, and that conclusion is: the organisation of speech in British secondary and further education classrooms is, at the very best, pathetic. While there are very good practitioners in every school and some colleges, the level of professional knowledge is little short of a deeply unfunny and really damaging joke.

The following opinion is unpopular with some. The fact that it is unpopular doesn't stop it being true. You may dislike this opinion. The visceral nature of your reaction does not stop it being true. There is a 'teaching technique' – a speaking and listening technique – that is used in more or less every lesson, in every school, in every county, in every country, in every single part of the known world; it is the default setting, the place we immediately grope for when managing a transition. It is the bedrock of AfL; maths teachers still believe in it; it is perceived by many teachers when they are starting out to be the very epitome and embodiment of teaching itself. No one in the world ever learned anything ever from being in the same room as this technique (apart, perhaps, from the fact that it doesn't work), and it creates about 50 per cent of the behaviour problems you will ever have in a

---

3   Do look out for *Everything I Know about Whipping*, E. O. Progress' next tome featuring pictures of the former secretary of state dressed in a scanty dominatrix outfit.

4   Yeh, I hate this word too. But I'd used 'evidence' in the next sentence and didn't want to utilise it twice. (And I hate utilise too. But I'd already utilised used.)

classroom. However, the fact that no one in the world ever learned anything ever from this technique does not stop it being the default setting of more or less every lesson, in every school, in every county, in every country, in every single part of the known world. It is a cancer on the raddled cheek of teaching and a blight on the life chances of the children in our classrooms.

What is it?

And you will know Satan by his many names. He is known as the teacher led discussion, he is known as questioning, he is known as 'guess what's in the teacher's head?', he is known as that bit where you stand at the front of the class and ask for contributions.

Why is it useless?

The same five kids make all the contributions.[5] The rest have worked out that if they just keep their eyes open they can be off in Majorca, or stealing a car, or pilfering objects from ladies' handbags.

What's the point?

It is rather more difficult to manage than you think when you enter the profession. It is physically exhausting. When the one kid who never talks finally

---

5   Yes, I know you can use lolly sticks. It doesn't stop the technique being pointless.

makes a contribution and it is totally wrong, and though you attempt to scaffold your response with praise before giving negative feedback, you've still told him he is wrong in front of his mates and you have still humiliated him. He never speaks again and retires hurt from education.

What's the point?

When there is heated debate it is impossible to manage. Hands up doesn't work. Many students are unable to assimilate this rule and blurt out contributions, leading you to publicly admonish, and it all kicks off.

What's the point?

The person doing most of the talking in a teacher led discussion, and therefore developing their oracy, is the teacher.

What's the point?

I'm glad you asked. There is no point.

There was an inevitability that this book would at some point have to brush up against the current ideological debate about traditional versus 'progressive' approaches. Aside from the observation that what the neotraditionals are attacking does not exist – I have never seen discovery learning in any classroom I have ever seen in twenty years – I would like to add a further contribution from the left of the field. Many of the teachers who espouse talking at kids, then asking them questions (and I speak here of the ring-leader of the tormentors, the blogger Andrew Old, who is quoted in this book, who I greatly like and think is an intelligent man and a serious thinker, but who I also think is wrong about a good few things), are maths teachers. Maths is a subject that stands alone: it has its own pedagogical disciplines and it is not language based, so maths teachers don't use the same amount of language, perhaps, as the subjects that are completely reliant on it. They also have to check understanding to a degree that is perhaps out of kilter with other subjects, as going on to the next part of the equation is entirely dependent on getting the last part right. Dylan Wiliam is a maths teacher. The techniques of questioning might be really useful for maths teachers. This doesn't make them relevant to everyone else.

DISPENSE WITH TEACHER LED DISCUSSION AND ORGANISE TALK IN MORE IMAGINATIVE WAYS

I have never tried to give up smoking. But I have given up biting my nails, which was easy; and I have also given up the teacher led discussion, which was far harder. It can take a couple of years of concerted effort to divest yourself of your addiction to teacher led discussion, as we are entirely conditioned to think of it as a valid technique, and in rejecting it we are having to act against our instinct to believe teaching's many truisms. You almost have to tie your hands behind your back in the early stages, but if you manage it, the benefits for your students are manifold.

The most beguiling aspect of Ian Gilbert's work, for me, has been the concept of "thought hand-grenades".[1] This concept, which Ian uses to describe the Thunks that he originated and that have made many a lesson, and indeed my own training, more interesting than it would otherwise have been, can be transferred so that it refers to any classroom activity in which the students talk to each other. Put 'em in pairs, threes, fours, sixes and throw stuff in for them to talk about. It's that simple. Put 'em in pairs and give 'em stuff to talk about; go from pairs to fours and get them to discuss what they discussed in

---

1   Ian Gilbert, *The Little Book of Thunks: 260 Questions to Make Your Brain Go Ouch!* (Carmarthen: Crown House Publishing, 2007), p. 21.

their first groups; have 'em in fours, separate them into twos and get them to talk about what they thought of the other pair's contribution. The grouping strategies are entirely dependent on the limits of your imagination and the limits of your research.

The key here is that you are not at the front talking and managing it; you are anywhere you fancy throwing stuff in. The point is that you no longer dominate the discussion[2] and you no longer develop your own skills of expression at the expense of the kids'. The same five kids don't dominate either. Everyone gets a go. Paired talk is best for this, as it ensures that everyone is taking a role. And, crucially, discussion must be in Standard English. You merely tour the class monitoring the discussion, checking for 'I was like(s)' and 'Yeh(s)' in an attempt to rid their formal expression of these curses; you also toss in new ideas and, if you are being reactive, new groupings. This work is totally differentiated, everyone can achieve something and everyone develops.

As for the groupings, just do a bit of research. I almost never see anything other than teacher led discussion, so I assume that many teachers are not familiar with the alternatives. If this means you, try out the following:

- Think – pair – share

- Think – pair – share – square

- Paired talk where you design the pairs

- Assigning roles within small groups

- Argument tunnel[3]

---

2   Why should you not do this? Well, read the essays they write after you have spent hours telling them what you think. Guess what? They are all the same. You have successfully indoctrinated a class into thinking what you have told them to think. Is it any wonder the neotrads are aligned to the right?

3   You can see this in action at: https://www.youtube.com/watch?v=zr2xdjQPH4I/.

- Jigsaws

As regards the stuff you throw in, well, obviously, subject specific is best, either as a starter before you've taught them some new stuff or, preferably, after you've taught them some new stuff so they get to practise using the new words you've taught them.

One of the people I've been most influenced by over the last decade is Gary Wilson, whose *Breaking the Barriers to Boys' Achievement* is a serious attempt to grapple with an impossible topic, and features many decent ideas and philosophies.[4] One of the highlights of the book is a table in which he outlines a variety of exercises in which students might profitably involve themselves in paired or grouped talk. His examples are delightful and include, "Invent a way of remembering where you live when you're drunk" and "What if there were no such thing as shoes?" What is interesting, though, is what happens when you take Gary's categories as they were intended and start to put them into a curricular context.

As an example, I'll use my own subject, English, and the most common novel formerly on the curriculum, *Of Mice and Men,* since, if you are under 40, you'll probably have been forced to read it at some point, against your will, and will have some piffling knowledge of it. If you don't, then don't worry. I have outlined an approach using Gary's headings, as well as the creative process a teacher might want to use if they are using his work to stimulate talk in a classroom.

---

4   Gary Wilson, *Breaking through Barriers to Boys' Achievement: Developing a Caring Masculinity* (London: Network Continuum, 2008).

Headings for speaking and listening activities		
The Reverse List ten things that would not have happened if Lennie didn't have learning difficulties.	**The Construction** Construct a design for the farm in which George and Lennie will live off "the fatta the land." Use the text to plot which animals live where.	**The Ridiculous** What would have been likely to happen if George had made a pass at Slim?
The What If? What if Curly was a decent and loving husband to his wife?	**The Variations** How many different ways does George protect Lennie?	**The Commonality** What do Slim and George have in common? What do Curly and Curly's wife have in common? What do Lennie and George have in common? What do Lennie and Crooks have in common?
The Disadvantages What are some of the disadvantages of being an itinerant farmhand in the dustbowl?	**The Picture** What connection does this picture tell you about life in the dustbowl?	**The Question** The answer is, "Because they were completely mutually dependent." What's the question?

The Combination	The Prediction	The Inventions
List what's good about Candy. Imagine a future in which Candy and Lennie become real friends. How would this help Lennie?	What will happen to George in the first hour after he has killed Lennie? What about the next month? Where will he be in four years' time?	Invent a way of remembering where you live when you're drunk.
The Alphabet	**The Different Uses**	**The Brick Wall**
Do an A–Z of emotions in *Of Mice and Men*.	List as many uses as possible for a man as strong as Lennie on a farm.	Consider what Candy or Crooks could do if either of them were sacked.

Adapted from Gary Wilson, *Breaking through Barriers to Boys' Achievement: Developing a Caring Masculinity* (London: Network Continuum, 2008), pp. 19–20.

You might get an immediate sense, if you were preparing for a serious analysis of this text, that you would be sketching over it a little: looking into corners where there is not much to pursue. That is not the point. The point is to get a holistic look at the subject from a variety of angles, and then come to a more mature understanding of it. Asking your students to talk about and record their responses and ideas to every one of these questions, particularly when it is applied specifically to an essay title or to a piece of pre-planning for some extended writing, generates great ideas. What's more, it allows students a full lesson in which they might generate those ideas through speaking to each other in Standard English.

ODD ONE OUT

"What's the odd one out between a car, a baby and a fridge?"

"It's obvious," says Charlie. "It's the baby."

"Why?" asks Sir.

"The other two are made of metal."

"How could it be the car?"

"Dunno."

"The other two are domestic, and you put milk in both of them. Cars don't live in houses, and if you put milk in them they don't like it," interjects Silas.

"Nice," Sir responds. "How could it be the fridge?"

"That's easy," Silas ejaculates. "The fridge is stationary; the baby and the car are ambulatory."

"I didn't know you knew that word."

"I don't, Sir. But since I don't actually exist, and am just a figment of your imagination, you can put any words you want in my mouth."

This activity is mildly geriatric, and you probably know it, but its potential value comes, again, when you locate it to subject specific questions. It's particularly useful for introducing skills of comparison and as prep for a comparative essay. Comparison is perceived to be a high order skill in British education, but, well, it isn't really: it's just spotting similarities and differences (what do they share and how are they different?), and this activity is useful for developing the ability to spot connections. If we go back to *Of*

Mice and Men, then we might ask a series of odd one out questions and get the students to discuss these in Standard English.

What's (or who's) the odd one out between:

- Crooks, Candy and Lennie?

- Sexism, misogyny and machismo?

- Homelessness, itinerancy and rootlessness?

- Friendship, love and co-dependency?

- Curly's wife, the ladies at the cathouse and Aunt Clara?

You can see here that what might initially appear to be quite a Noddy activity can actually prompt discussion and analysis of some fairly high order concepts. The discussions might prompt work of a higher intellectual level than just sitting individually and writing down your own thoughts; it encourages fine distinction and leads to quality thought and well-articulated expression of the same.

The first time I did this activity with a group of students was in the East End, and we had a new student who had arrived freshly that week from Poland. Seated in a circle, I asked the boys, "Who is the odd one out between Shakespeare, Banquo and Lady Macbeth?" Quick as a fox doing a passable impersonation of a short legged Usain Bolt, Lukasz piped up in a heavily accented voice, "Banquo, Sir: ze other two are totally over-ambitious." Which was greeted with general assent round da circle, "New Polish kid is proper clever, innit?"

BABBLE GABBLE

This is a technique I nicked off a primary practitioner some time back. You get the kids into pairs and get them to name one of them A and one of them B. B gets the nice job initially. Inform them that for the next one-and-a-half minutes all you want them to do is some lovely doodling – and even that is not compulsory. Alternatively, they might want to try a thought experiment and see if it's possible to think of nothing at all for a minute-and-a-half – and even that is not compulsory – they might want to just close their eyes and have a brief nap at this point. A gets the difficult job. They have to spend a period of time scribing down, in note form, everything they know about a particular subject: plate tectonics, long division, the reign of James I, anything. After the requisite time has elapsed, and you've woken up the narcoleptic kid,[5] you run the following script:

RightnowAyou'vegottospeakasfastasyoupossiblycanandtellBeverythi
ngyouknowabouteverythingyouknowaboutthesubject:platetectonics,
longdivision,thereignofJamesIwhatever.

Once this has run its course, you manage the transition and mouth the following further instruction:

BspeakingfasterthanAspoketoyoucouldyourepeatbackeverythingyou-
canrememberthatAsaidtoyouaboutthesubject:platetectonics,longdiv
ision,thereignofJamesIwhatever.

---

5   I once taught a sweet narcoleptic boy in Ramsgate. He fell asleep, I covered him up with his coat. It repeated.

There is a further stage which is worth trying out here, again with a scripted instruction:

AspeakingfasterthanBspoketoyouwhentheywererepeatingwhatyou-saidtothemcanyounowpointoutanyinaccuraciesorinconsistenciesin-whatBsaidtoyouwhentheywererepeatingwhatyousaidtothem.

In truth, this activity is more for fun than for any real concrete learning. What is interesting about it, however, is that it is profoundly cognitively stretching (and, as such, it might not be just for fun). If you doubt this, try it yourself. Your cogs have to be whirring really bloody quickly to get this right.

NOT ENOUGH EXTENDED WRITING ANYWHERE, EVER

The son to whom this book is dedicated, Leonard, and I played a game for years every Friday after he had returned from a week in the warm, soft hands of the primary school he attended. It was in the form of a repetitive dialogue in which the script was exactly the same every week, but which we'd try to add different intonations in order to keep it relatively fresh. The script went like this:

Dad: Len, have you got any homework?

Len: Yes, Dad. I have got some homework.

(The school were rigorous in sending home photocopied sheets of paper with some writing on them.[1])The conversation continued …

Dad: Len, is it a healthy eating poster?

Len: Yes, Dad. How did you guess? It is a healthy eating poster.

The result of my beautiful and brilliant son receiving countless homework tasks to make a poster advertising eating healthily has been salutary. They have affected his taste in food not a jot; he would still subsist on a diet of crisps and sweets if left unsupervised. However, there has been an

---

1   Though I am legally obliged to note here that they have made some quite substantial improvements in a lot of areas over the last few years.

unintended result: Len is accidentally, absolutely, completely and utterly brilliant at creating healthy eating posters. He is intimate with every nuance; delicate and exacting in his understanding of what constitutes an appropriate image; judiciously experimental in his choice of typeface. We have even tried an experiment in which he did one blindfolded, with crayons, with his feet: the results were barely credible. He wasn't as good at writing as someone of his intelligence should have been at the age of 11. He hadn't had much practice, you see.[2]

Many of the end of unit examinations through which our students' validity and potential are assessed come in the form of extended writing activities. They will do better at writing a validly argued piece of prose if they are allowed attempts in which they are permitted to experiment and play, and to make the mistakes through which they will learn.

Another story that resonates with me is related to a friend of mine whom I don't see enough of, as the rent's always got to be paid. His name is Chris Roberts, and if you know anything at all about rock journalism then you will know he is the greatest of all time. (If you think you know anything at all about rock journalism and think someone else is a better writer, then you know nothing about rock journalism.) The issue with being the greatest rock writer of all time, and particularly of the late 1980s and early 1990s (when he was really in his pomp), is that it was a great job; it is not such a great job now. Chris likens it to being a coal miner: there are no mines any more and, similarly, there are very few outlets that cover music in a serious enough manner to pay even great writers paltry rates. The industry is gone.

While Chris' career recently has hit something of an Indian summer – he has published books on Kate Moss and Gothic subculture this year alone – a few years ago he was forced (by me) to apply for a job in education. Much to

---

2   Though I would like to put on record my respect for and gratitude to Jez Pinfold, of the English department at Forest Hill School for boys, whose professionalism and talent has transformed my son's experience of education.

our mutual surprise he was invited to interview, and contacted me in a panic having not the first idea of what goes on in the dizzying realm of the professional educator. "Relax, Chris," I said. "Come round to mine and I'll brief you."

In my front room, I gave him a piece of advice that, at the time I was saying it, felt like it made sense. "At some point during the interview," I advised smugly, "and it will help if you are slightly glib here, look the interviewer in the eye and state the following phrase, 'Of course, people only ever learn through a process of practice and review.' If the interviewer is female, it may help if you wink at this point. You are still an attractive man."

Chris spluttered a question in response, "Are all teachers stupid?"

"Why?"

"Because everyone knows this. Really, you are presenting this to me as some kind of holy jewel, but everyone, everywhere, outside of educational institutions, it seems, knows that you learn through a process of practice and review. What have I been doing for the last thirty years? Watching the performance of virtuosic musicians. What did they all have in common? They practised. Strewth! I thought you were bright."

Chris is right. We get better at something through doing it, then from having an expert guiding us through how to improve the next time we play the same piece, or through a process of self-assessment. It seems that this message still hasn't filtered down to some schools which are of the mind that their students will make great strides in literacy without ever being asked to write anything more complex than transcribing a waferish slogan on a healthy eating poster.

DO LOTS OF DIFFERENT VARIETIES OF WRITING

Ros Wilson refers to one of the issues with writing across the curriculum as being the preponderance of "dry, expository forms". The write-up of the science experiment, the description of the processes that go to form a scree slope, the analysis of Weimar Germany are all in the form of a report in formal impersonal language. This form of writing is an important skill to inculcate in students, but it is rarely a lot of fun until you have reached the point of mastery when you can develop a waspish tone; and this is not something primary aged kids are going to acquire at the same time as they are focused on learning how to tie up their own shoelaces.

One of the ways around this is a means of defining task that English teachers use in a fairly unthinking and uncritical way: that of defining the purpose, the audience and the genre of the writing. You might, if you were feeling lazy and wanted a rapid solution to making writing across the curriculum more imaginative, want to use the following template:

For this exercise you must first define the subject, specific to your own curriculum area, that you want to teach:

Write it here.

Now identify the genre of writing that you are going to ask your students to do. Circle one of the following (perhaps the more absurd the text type seems, the more entertainment you and your students will have):

anecdote, apology, autobiography, biography, book review, cartoon, character sketch, comic strip, complaint, description, diary entry, editorial, essay, eulogy, explanation, fable, fairy tale, fantasy, how-to-do-it article, interview, joke or riddle, legend, letter, list, magazine article, monologue, news article, pamphlet, parody, persuasive letter, play, poem, proposal, report, résumé, retelling, review, satire, science fiction, short story, song, speech, TV script, commercial, thank you note, tongue twister, wanted poster

Now identify a purpose for the writing. Circle one of the following:

to express feelings, to explore, to entertain, to inform, to explain, to instruct, to describe, to argue for, to argue against, to persuade, to evaluate, to mediate, to negotiate a solution

Now identify an audience for the writing

Age

Gender

Education

Economic status

Political/social/religious beliefs

Level of information they have about the subject (novice, general reader, specialist or expert)

Having defined the purpose, audience and genre, you must now brainstorm what you would have to teach your students before the writing task in order for them to properly fulfil it.

This appears useful. However, the issue with defining purpose, audience and genre is that one of these things is entirely pointless. Which one?[1] The useful stuff here is in the list of different genres.

---

1   Audience. If you think about this, there are only really two different ways of writing for differing audiences: formal or informal: 'writing up' or 'writing down'. Since our students are only ever really going to be assessed on their ability to 'write up' there is no point in teaching them to 'write down'. It is the manifold habits of 'writing down' that we are actually trying to exorcise.

REINTRODUCE STORY TIME IN PRIMARY SCHOOLS

The second solution is specifically directed at primary schools, and is as nostalgic as much of Mr Gove's approach to education policy. When I was a little boy, the first thing we did every morning at primary school was to spend an hour writing stories. We didn't know we were learning anything; it was just a piece of fun and a nice, quiet way to settle into the day. My own children do not do this, and I think the result of the literacy hour from yonks ago is that students now spend a lot of time on decontextualised grammar worksheets, but do not actually have much time in the day to demonstrate their learning though extended pieces of writing. An hour's story time every morning would radicalise their writing. It seems a counterproductive shame that young children are not given sufficient licence to play with words any more.

MARKING NOT BEING TAKEN ANYWHERE NEAR SERIOUSLY ENOUGH

The research is pretty clear: decent formative feedback is the intervention which is most key to student improvement. It comes at the top of every table of effect sizes and counts even more than prior student attainment (how clever your students are) and teacher quality (how good your lessons are).

If you want your students to improve give them plenty of advice about how they might do so. Otherwise, how will they know? This applies equally to literacy as to any other subject, and particularly to writing. So, if the argument that assessment is worth doing as well as it is possible to do it has prevailed, where is the problem?

Let's try seeing what *you* think. Put yourself in the shoes of a parent of one of your students. How often do they think that you should mark their child's work?

Be honest.

If you are a parent answer the question yourself: how often should your child's book or work be marked? If you are not a parent, then try and imagine yourself as one.

Be honest.

Do not be affected by your own experiences as a teacher.

If you were honest you may have come up with what parents really think, which is: "Every day. I expect my son's book marked every day. I do not see this as an unreasonable expectation, and no parent I have ever met sees it as so. If you do not mark whatever my son writes, then you are not doing your job properly and should be sacked."

OK. Let's look at it through another prism – your own eyes. How many class sets of work/books do you think it is reasonable for your SLT/ALT to call you on? What should the minimum expectation be in terms of how many class sets you should be expected to mark in a day?

The best answer to this that I have heard, and the one that best sums up the consensus around the country, from a teacher in Stourbridge, is "One ... but with a lower case 'o'."

Most teachers think that it is reasonable to expect them to mark a full class set of book each working day. As a full time classroom teacher, I was a zealot about marking, and would rise at 4.30 a.m. so that I could be in school as it opened. I was match fit, mustard keen, at the top of my marking form and had an AST's preferential timetable. At my very best, I could manage two class sets of books a day, and in doing so wrecked my health, my ability to last a half-term without going down with something and jeopardised my important human relationships.

So, an ambitious zealot with no real sense of what is realistic to ask of himself can manage two class sets a day for a limited period. Let's look at the NQT music teacher who has landed in a classroom where the only instruments are drums (and, gawd, once they are out even a morning becomes completely unmanageable in terms of retaining sanity) and the only resources in the cupboard are lots of tatty photocopied worksheets about Bob Marley. He has five free periods a week and has to teach five periods each day, all of which have some kind of written outcome. If he is a zealot he is still going to leave three class sets each day unmarked. If he is a zealot he is still going to be fighting an uphill battle in which he is losing way more than he wins. But he is not a zealot, he is just a nice young man doing his best, and, as a result, he is leaving four class sets a day unmarked.

IT DOES NOT ADD UP. IT DOES NOT ADD UP.

It does not add up. It has never added up. They are lying to us. Ofsted expect teachers to mark five or six class sets of books a day. Ofsted inspectors were completely unable to mark five class sets of books a day when they were

111

teachers. They are lying to us, and they know they are lying to us. It cannot be done.

Here is a picture of a pint glass.

How much does it hold? Yes, that's right. A pint. What happens when you attempt to pour four extra pints into it when it is already working at full capacity? It goes all over the floor, making a horrific mess that someone will have to spend a lot of time mopping up.

So it is with marking: you are already working at full capacity. Government agencies or management teams telling you that you have more capacity and are not just not working hard enough does not change the fundamental truth of this. The question occurs then: if we accept that quality formative feedback is the key to student attainment, and we all want to be the best teacher we can possibly be, but we are already working at full capacity, how do we ensure that our students receive as much of it as possible?

USE CREATIVE APPROACHES TO FORMATIVE ASSESSMENT AND FEEDBACK

USE WORD COUNTS

I made a mistake in my NQT year of setting an unthinking homework off the top of my head on a Friday; hastily mumbling, "Year 7, could you just write me a lovely fairy story over the weekend" had an unintended consequence. I still recall Vicky's look of glee, and my own look of horror, as she bounced in on chubby little legs having filled a whole exercise book with a fairy story using character names from *EastEnders* ("And Prince Beppe said to Princess Tiffany ...") and not a single paragraph break. Marking that was a long dark week of the soul. From that point I came up with a strategy to ensure it never, ever happened again.

A question: what would be the consequences of having a school policy where every piece of written work came with a word count?

Think about it in this space.

There are interesting outcomes here. First, let me tell you something you should already know: every single professional piece of writing ever commissioned comes with both a word count and a deadline. An editor will ask for 600 words on a particular subject by Wednesday. My columns for *The Guardian* were always 1,000 words long, as they had to fill a specific space. If every single professional piece of writing ever commissioned comes with a word count, then why are we not asking our students to imagine a future and develop the skills that they might use if they were to consider writing professionally? If it's good enough for the pros, then it's good enough for your students or mine.

When you first introduce this strategy, a variety of outcomes occur. First, when you ask for 100 words the kids say, en masse, their own regional form of, "Nah man, 100 words is a long ting." And they remain of such mind until they have completed the task, when they realise, "100 words isn't such a long ting, innit? Now 250 words, dat would be a long ting." The benefit of this is that you can outline exactly the length of the piece of writing you want, and the students soon get hip to how much writing the various numbers signify (100 words is a paragraph, 250 words a page). They are therefore gifted the solution to the empty page staring at them. One of the issues with undertaking an open ended writing task is that you don't know when it will be over. You could be entering a triathlon that will never finish, and it is this that makes the starting of the task quite so difficult and so dispiriting. The blank page stares. You don't start. If you are aware where the end is likely to be, and just how much effort you are going to have to put in, then starting is easier.

It also teaches the skills of brevity and clarity: if you only have an allotted period in which to say what you have to say, then you'd better be on point. Furthermore, it teaches the writerly skill of bumping up the word count with superfluous, unnecessary, pointless adjectives (all hack writers do this), and it makes the task cognitively stimulating and creative in a way it wouldn't have been without the word count.

Crucially, though, if you institute word counts you can manage your marking burden. Did ya hear me? You can manage your marking burden! I'm not kidding ya! You will never be in the position where a student writes so much that you have to spend all evening lovingly poring over one book with a hot red pen. If you want to assess one piece of knowledge, ask them to write a twenty word sentence about it or a thirteen word sentence. This has the additional benefit of getting students thinking about sentence length and the rhythm of their writing.

Another way of managing your marking burden is asking yourself the fairly honest question as to how much of the writing in your class is merely ritualistic. There's an easy way of checking this: have a look at the exercise book of a kid in your class. If there is a series of entries where there is a title and date, copied objective and perhaps key words, and nothing else, then there was no point whatsoever in you getting the book out of the cupboard. Leave them there until you have a written task that will engage them in thought and practice. And shed yourself of the idea that a lesson with no written outcome is in any way a doss. It isn't. You do not have to have a pen in your hand to learn. You can spend weeks without one and learn loads. Try to plan a whole week of lessons in which there is no written outcome whatsoever for four of your classes. See how it affects the quality of written feedback that your other classes receive.

On this (whisper it): not all feedback has to be in written form. Management teams prefer peachily kept and rigorously marked books, as it provides an easily observable audit trail that they can show to the bottom inspectors when they arrive every four years. But if you think about your own area of professional expertise, you will be proudly aware that you are able to see three areas in which your student might improve on just glancing at their first paragraph. It is the scribing of the comments that takes all the time in marking. Solution: don't do it.

Buy yourself a 'verbal feedback given' stamp online. Get into work early and catch up with your marking by just stamping every single piece of work. Award yourself two gold stars for initiative and don't forget to ring in sick tomorrow.[1]

Actually, the idea is that you feed back to the student, verbally, in lessons, providing them with three targets for improvement, which they then transcribe into their exercise books themselves. "Yes, you do the donkey work. See how you like it?" Et voilà, you have an audit trail, your students have received quality feedback and you still have some of your hair and many of your teeth.

TECHNICAL STUFF

There are a further couple of things that are well worth knowing as regards marking. First, why do you think you should number their targets? So you can refer back to them in the next piece of marking, and they can be used as a criteria for what you are looking for in the next piece.

The second point should be common knowledge, but I am saddened that when I tell teachers about it many of them have never encountered this piece of information. Wiliam and Black's research has revealed conclusively that you can spend night after night scrabbling through hundreds of books, lovingly scribing them with the sweetest of positive comments, then following these with numbered targets that are at once technical and spiritual, and

---

1   This reminds me of a former colleague of whom I asked, on returning from the Christmas hols, whether he had managed to mark all the mocks I'd sweated over so punctiliously during yuletide. "Nope," he replied. "I just chucked them in the bin and gave them the grades I thought they'd get." He is now a head teacher.

it will all have been for no reason if you put a grade on the work.[2] Formative and summative are – to an extent – distinct. Yes, you can use summative tasks for formative means (i.e. finding out what the class do not know), but they should not receive their grades and their comments simultaneously. There are probably easy ways to circumvent this: for example, when a piece has two functions, give them their feedback at the beginning of the lesson and their grades at the end.

A FINAL WORD

My son, Len, is aware of what I do for a living, and gave me a message four years ago to pass on to every teacher I work with. It relates to flick and tick. I'll let Len speak his thoughts:

> You know that marking that you do like this [Len puts his hand over his eyes so that he cannot see at all]? Well, this is what it says to us [starts miming ticking the air with his other hand]: "I haven't read this piece of work [mimes initialling the bottom of it] and I don't care about you."

Len was 8 when he told me this.

---

2 Paul Black and Dylan Wiliam, 'Assessment and Classroom Learning', *Assessment in Education* 5(1) (1998): 7–74.

WELL-MEANING IDIOTS TELLING KIDS THAT SPELLING ISN'T IMPORTANT

Here we are in the realm, yet-a-bloody-gain, of rules for one thing being conflated with another. It is arguably an entirely reasonable piece of professional behaviour to tell a young person grappling with dyslexia that spelling doesn't necessarily affect whether their writing is legible. It is arguably an entirely reasonable thing to say, "It's OK. The spelling doesn't really matter in terms of whether I can read it or not." However, a clever teacher made a particularly salient point recently in the form of a question: "Who in the room is spelling most important to?" Yes, that's right. The dyslexic kid. You could therefore argue that even if this piece of exceptional advice for a student with a specific learning difficulty is well-intentioned, and there is truth in it, it would be better for the dyslexic child if you taught them how to spell.

This particular piece of advice is useless and damaging for mainstream kids, as it affects the urgency and seriousness with which they approach this fundamental part of literacy. What do you personally think when you see a spelling error in a school newsletter, some teaching materials, a newspaper? You think the person responsible is an indiot [*sic*]. There are some lovely examples of this on the web: the school that had a sign outside saying, "Our Teachers Make a Differance"; the local newspaper headline which informed its readers, "County Spelling Bee Postoned One More Time"; and, finally and brilliantly, the teenage boy with a huge tattoo on his back informing the world, "Only God Can Juge Me", which is not entirely true now, is it? Imagine you are looking over job applications and you receive one with no spelling errors and one with a number of them. Which are you likely to look upon more favourably? The former, clearly.

The question is, how big a problem is this? And the answer is best answered, as is my house style, with a series of quasi-amusing anecdotes. I worked as a consultant last year with a good school with some very good teachers indeed. I did a day of observations focusing on their approaches to literacy in order to design a training intervention that was specific to their needs and would support their improvement. I saw loads of really good practice in this school and some genuinely inspiring and extremely professional teachers. Spelling in the school, however, was little short of horrifying. Spelling errors on the board, made by post-graduate teachers, included 'realy', 'independance' and 'refering'; teaching materials featured errors of the magnitude of 'proffesional'. Also, as is sadly the case in many schools, teachers outside of the English department did not ordinarily correct spellings in books. This gives implicit authority to students to continue misspelling those words. The following misspellings were left uncorrected:

Subject area	Misspelling errors
Science	safty, mateirials, moveing, differant, assement, eviroment, habiat (these last two were both ticked as correct spellings)
Humanities	somokeing, dicintergrated, cigarates, centry

This practice was observed in an extremely good school, with some great teachers, that has subsequently gone on to make real improvements which have been endorsed by the lesson observer pursuivants. What would a book check reveal regarding whether misspelling is left uncorrected in your school? In your department? In your class? It is not just the English department's job. What is the point of the poor English teacher, whose marking burden makes yours look like a 5-year old's, correcting every misspelling they encounter when you and the rest of your department leave them uncorrected? None. You are undermining your colleague, undermining the kids' ability to achieve and perhaps even their ability to get a job. Get your red pen out and start correcting.

I was working in a school in Yorkshire last year. It was a bugger of a commute, but if I got up at 3.30 a.m. I could be there for period 1. The fascinating thing about this school – in which I genuinely heard a child utter the phrase, "Tilly Trimble got caught with chuddy down the snicket" – was that half of the kids couldn't spell their own names. This was not their fault; it was the fault of the parents who had all spelled them wrongly on the birth certificate and weren't sufficiently literate to spot their own error. I taught a class full of lovely kids whose names included Zannya, Callum, Kiera, Lucie and Zak. A catalogue of errors.

(There's a further story related to names which I'll share here, just because I like it. The story of Nivek: bottle blonde, and reputedly in possession of 'attitude', but perfectly charming if you spoke to her like the intelligent human she was. Her name though remained mystical, and I had thought her to be of Polish extraction. I spoke to John, the head, about the Polish girl, thinking to report how much I liked her and how bright and how nice she was for someone who had a reputation for being challenging.

"What Polish girl?" he asked.

"The one with the blonde hair. Nivek? Nivek: that's a Polish name, isn't it?"

"On no," replied John. "She's not Polish. Her father called her that because he wanted a boy."

"I'm sorry, I don't see the significance."

"He'd really gone to town with imagining having a boy."

"Sorry … And?"

"A boy he could call the same name as himself."

"Nivek? He's Polish then."

"No. His name's Kevin. He was really disappointed she wasn't a boy. It's Kevin backwards."

There's no point to this anecdote. Other than the fact that I have longed to get it into a book for five years, and the chance has never presented itself. Until now.)

Ultimately, though, the issue is that the products our schools are producing, the factories' outcomes, so to speak, can't spell. Not only is this an issue for the kids, but it also plays into the hands of the CBI who, year on year, publish a report moaning about the literacy skills of the young people they encounter. This gives policy makers the moral authority to tamper with British schools, increase your workload and dock your pension. If we are not to up our game for the young people we serve (and this is sad), then let's do it for our own sake. It's difficult to defend an education system that leaves over half of its kids unable to spell.

Let's start this process of upping our game with a look at why it's such a problem.

WHY IS SPELLING SO DIFFICULT?

For this we've got to go all the way back to the roots of the language. English is thought to have originated from a specific little part of the bit of Jutland that isn't Denmark: the Angeln peninsula of the Schleswig-Holstein region of Germany. We speak a language that a German tribe originated before they decided it might be a good idea to pack their coracles with lederhosen, cured meat products and their superior knowledge of brewing techniques, and see if there was anything over the other side of the water. Nothing at all was written down in English until the sixth century, when the Church, expansionist and proselytising as ever, decided that they could better spread the 'good news' if they could write things down rather than going and convincing the peasants to bow down before them and their invisible friend on a face-to-face basis. The clergy made the not unreasonable decision to use an existing alphabet to write it down with: the Roman alphabet. However, if you look at the Roman alphabet below, and compare it to the English alphabet, a few things will jump out at you.

A	B	C	D	E	F	G
H	I	K	L	M	N	O
P	Q	R	S	T	V	X
Y	Z					

There are three letters missing: 'j', 'u' and 'w'. ('J' is basically just an 'i' at the front of a word, and the 'u' and 'w' are explained in a lengthy and boring footnote at the bottom of this page.[1]) Furthermore, there were certain sounds in spoken English that did not correspond with any of the sounds the Roman alphabet could muster, such as the 'th' sound. They didn't have that sound in Latin. And whereas, historically, Londoners have come up wiv the proper elegant solution of doing away wiv da sound entirely, dis was not good enough for the Anglo-Saxon missionaries, and dey got to finking. Initially, their solution was to import a couple of signs from the runic alphabet: 'eth' (which looks like a runic 'd') and 'thorn' (which looks like a runic 'p'). 'Thorn' was used predominantly in the south and 'eth' (or 'daet') in the north. But by the eighth century they became interchangeable, although 'thorn' was used more at the beginning of words and 'eth' at the end.[2]

Eventually, having two different signifiers for the same sound became a bit of a bore, even for people used to listening to their own sermons, and the emissaries of the kirk came up with a lasting solution: the digraph (putting two letters together to signify a sound). And that's why the 'ch' sound in chicken, which is one sound, is actually signified by two letters; likewise, the 'sh' in sherry and, of course, the 'th' in thimbleful. It is the existence of digraphs that makes our language difficult to read and difficult to spell. As language expert David Crystal writes, "forty+ phonemes with twenty-six letters? That, in a nutshell, is the problem of English spelling."[3]

---

1   Why do the Poles drink wodka? Is it that the Russians deliberately made it really cheap during the communist years in order to destroy Polish masculinity? Or is it because, in Latin, the sound the 'w' is doing was performed by the 'v'? Furthermore, in Middle English the 'u' and the 'v' were interchangeable: that's why the letter we call a double 'u' actually looks like a double 'v'. Interesting, no?

2   Interestingly, 'thorn' is still used in the Icelandic alphabet, which can cause some difficulties when you're asking directions to what you think is called Pingviller!

3   David Crystal, *Spell It Out: The Singular Story of English Spelling* (London: Profile, 2012), p. 19.

So, not only is it difficult to spell in English, it is difficult to read as well. This has been further compounded by the existence of shwoahing.[4]

SHWOAHING

I learned to read with Peter and Jane books through a technique called whole word guessing. I got really good at it. I came back from my first day at school convinced that I didn't need to go again. "No, it's alright, Mum, I can read now. Look. 'Here is Peter. Here is Jane. Here is Peter and Jane. Here is Pat the dog.' I can even do it without the book. (Closes book) 'Here is Peter. Here is Jane. Here is Peter and Jane. Here is Pat the dog.'" And still she sent me to school the next day. Eventually, because so many people were left illiterate by whole word guessing, it was felt that it might be a good idea to teach kids the sounds the letters made. But for years they were teaching them the wrong sounds, and it all went to cock. As an illustration, imagine yourself as 4 again. You are being taught to read.

Teacher: What does this letter say? (Holds up flashcard with a 'C' on it)

Student: Cuh.

Teacher: Correct. Well done. What does this letter say? (Holds up flashcard with an 'A' on it)

Student: Ahh.

Teacher: Correct. Well done. What does this letter say? (Holds up flashcard with an 'T' on it)

---

4   Primary teachers look away now. You know all this stuff. You'll be amazed to find that almost no secondary teacher does.

Student: Tuh.

Teacher: Correct. Well done. Now put them together. What does it say?

Student: Cuhahhtuh … Cuhahhtuh … Cuhahhtuh.

Teacher: No. It says cat.

Student: Well, that's bollocks, Miss. It doesn't sound anything like cat. It sounds like cuhahhtuh.

Shwoahing was the flawed technique with which teachers would advise kids that the consonants had an 'uh' on the end when you sounded them out. It stopped a lot of people reading. The real sounds of consonants are more clipped. The 'c' and the 't' sounds are almost entirely percussive; the 'l' sound isn't 'luh', it's 'ull'; the 'r' sound isn't 'ruh', it's 'urr'; the 'w' sound isn't 'wuh', it's 'oo' (really).

Once this was fixed, another problem became evident: that of vowel digraphs. We'll go back to teaching the 4-year-old. The teacher and student now know they shouldn't shwoah, so it should all be plain sailing.

Teacher: What does this letter say? (Holds up flashcard with a 'B' on it)

Student: Buh.[5]

Teacher: Correct. Well done. What does this letter say? (Holds up flashcard with an 'O' on it)

Student: Orh.

Teacher: Correct. Well done. What does this letter say? (Holds up flashcard with an 'A' on it)

---

5   It's almost impossible not to shwoah a little bit on 'B' and 'D': the dumbkopfs of the alphabet.

Student: Ah.

Teacher: Correct. Well done. What does this letter say? (Holds up flashcard with an 'T' on it)

Student: T.

Teacher: Correct. Well done. Now put them together. What does it say?

Student: Buhorhaht ... Buhorhaht ... Buhorhaht.

Teacher: No. It says boat.

Student: What utter cack! It doesn't sound anything like boat. It sounds like buhorhaht. Where in God's name did they get you from? You're useless.

This has all been solved by a lovely little rhyme invented by those brilliant people who came up with Jolly Phonics, and that rhyme is, "When two vowels go walking, the first one does the talking, and it says its own name." Basically, in a vowel digraph, all the second vowel is doing is tapping its cousin on the shoulder and telling it to say its name. So, in 'tie' all the 'e' is doing is tapping the 'i' on the shoulder and saying, "Say your name, cousin." In 'tea' all the 'a' is doing is tapping the 'e' on the shoulder and saying, "Say your name, cousin." In 'glee' all the second 'e' is doing is tapping the first one on the shoulder and saying, "What's our name, bruv?"

This goes further into the realms of what primary practitioners call the "magic 'e'". This is where there is an 'e' at the end of the word, which is separated from previous vowels by a consonant. All the final 'e' is doing is reaching over the consonant and tapping the previous vowel on the shoulder, asking him to say his name. Final and definitive proof, therefore, that 85 per cent of you pronounce this word entirely incorrectly: scone. The magic 'e' in 'scone' is merely telling the previous 'o' to says its name. I will not enter into any correspondence about this, but should you wish to meet outside a pub, sans glasses, to defend your right to pronounce it like a snob, then be aware I am prepared to go all the way and will do whatever it takes.

ERM, TEACH THEM TO SPELL

How many words are there in the English language? David Crystal advises that there are over a million, and an estimate by the Global Language Monitor on 1 January 2014 had it that there were 1,025,109.[1] Whatever the real number, and it doesn't really matter, what we can conclude is that if, like most primary school classes, we learn fifteen separate spellings a week, then, given a forty week academic year, it would take us in the region of 16,000 years to learn all of them, and, really, we just don't have the time.

It behoves us, therefore, to equip our students with some strategies with which they might be able to learn how to spell correctly or, at least, as correctly as they are able to. The most obvious and hoary of these is the primary school banker: 'look – say – cover – write – check'. This is the technique most beloved of those institutions which set weekly spelling lists for small children to learn. If you are not familiar with this then you are probably what is known in certain circles as a 'secondary school teacher'. In which case it is a useful technique to have in your armoury, particularly for learning the spellings of key vocabulary, either on a weekly basis or at the beginning/end of a unit of work.

Primaries generally use 'look – say – cover – write – check' to send home spellings that must be learned and which you will be tested on next Friday. The principle is as easy as the title. You look at the spelling, say it out loud (which can get you odd looks on the bus, as the stream of non sequiturs that

---

1   See http://www.languagemonitor.com/number-of-words/
    number-of-words-in-the-english-language-1008879/.

this causes you to utter in sequence will have you labelled as mad), cover over the correct spelling, write your idea of the spelling in the appropriate space, then uncover and check if you've spelled it correctly.

Below is an example of difficult words to spell from the mid-to-later realms of the alphabet. Even if you can't be bothered to sully the book, you can see, in principle, that it is really just daily practice and that it'd probably work. The specific benefit for this in secondary schools is that you can justify it as a homework. Setting a weekly spelling test in science, for example, will have you marked out as 'doing something' about literacy that ticks a box and excuses you from having to take on board any of the more challenging aspects of the recommendations in this book. If you are going to sully the book, then today is Friday.

	Monday	Tuesday	Wednesday	Thursday	Friday
Mnemonic					
Occasion					
Occurrence					
Onomatopoeia					
Paradigm					
Pronunciation					

Other than the obvious, it's worth a brief diversion into the magical world of spelling to look at some of the many myths that surround it. Much of this comes from the best book ever written about spelling for practitioners, *Unscrambling Spelling* by Cynthia Klein and Robin R. Millar, which is mystifyingly out of print, and can, if the wind has changed, set you back sixty quid or so on Amazon. It is actually worth the money, as there are few people who have thought as deeply about spelling as these authors, and to misquote Margaret Thatcher on Keith Joseph, where other books list the problems, this brings you the solutions. In one section, it lists many of the commonly held myths (or not myths) about spelling, which are worth a look at.[2] I'll briefly examine these. Bear in mind, please, that these are my own inexpert responses to the 'myths' and that if you want the real answer you will have to stump up the £60 or so it costs to read what a real expert thinks.

If you want to learn to spell you should read more

Here we are back, yet again, to the children's author view of literacy: the conflation of one skill (reading: an act of decoding) with another (spelling: an element of writing, a process of encoding). Of course, reading is of value in itself, and perhaps, if you are wired in the standard manner, then reading more will have you encountering new words and re-encountering the correct spellings of partially familiar words. But it ain't necessarily so. You may not be wired in the standard way. It is possible that you will be a voracious reader and excited consumer of stories, but will have a spelling specific version of dyslexia. It is more usual than not that you will not learn by some magical process of osmosis, but will need to be taught, and that merely

---

2   Cynthia Klein and Robin R. Millar, *Unscrambling Spelling* (London: Hodder & Stoughton, 1990), Resource Sheet 2, p. 43.

chucking books at you will teach you little aside from the fact that you dislike having books chucked at you.

There's no logic in English spelling; that's why it's so hard

There is some logic to this, but that logic is pretty arcane. The oft quoted, "Though the rough cough and hiccough plough me through, I ought to cross the lough," which has a huge number of variations of the pronunciation of the 'ou' digraph, is revealed by David Crystal to have come from a multiplicity of sources.[3] The 'gh' sounded as 'f' is actually an Americanism, as it was coined/created by the gent, Noah Webster, who came up with the first American dictionary in 1828; the 'ou' sound in 'cough' is a short 'o' sound; hiccough was originally spelled 'hickup', but was deliberately changed so that it looked like its not at all related bodily function, the 'cough'; in 'plough' the French 'gh' is used, and sounds like 'ow'; 'though' was originally 'thoz' and has evolved from there; and the pronunciation in 'lough' is Gaelic. There's a reason for everything, you know, and some logic too. But it's not always easy to see.

---

3   David Crystal, *How Language Works: How Babies Babble, Words Change Meaning and Languages Live or Die* (New York: Penguin, 2005), p. 130.

People make spelling mistakes because they don't speak properly

Sadly, there's some mileage in this. If you have a working class or regional accent, then this can impact on your spelling. Similarly, if you speak a dialect form this may impact on the words you choose. In South London, for instance, we have managed to reduce the question, "What is the matter with you?" to "Smatter?" The latter spelling is frowned on in polite circles.

If a child gets stuck on spellings they should just sound it out

The best spelling error of all time came from sounding it out. That error is Chuckyembrosward. I'll leave you to figure it out by giving you the context, "Dis summer I 'av been studding for my Chuckyembrosward."[4] If you consider the absurd, arcane logic outlined in the section on there being no logic in English spelling above, you can come up with a pretty watertight argument that this isn't always going to work in all situations.

If you learn the rules you'll be able to spell

The issue being, of course, that many of the rules are nonsense. If we look at the most famous, "'i' before 'e', except after 'c'", whatever the Department for Education was called in 2009, they were fairly categorical about its use,

---

4   It is the Duke of Edinburgh's Award.

The i before e after c rule is not worth teaching. It applies only to words in which the ie or the ei stands for a clear /ee/ sound and unless this is known words such as sufficient, veil and their look like exceptions. There are so few words where the ei spelling for the /ee/ sound follows the letters c that it is easier to spell the specific words: receive, conceive, deceive (+ the related words receipt, conceit, deceit), perceive and ceiling.[5]

And if you do the tiniest bit of research into how many words have the 'e' before the 'i' (seize, forfeit, heinous, neighbour, leisure, weigh, seize, vein, eight, veil, beige, rein, weird, heir, reign, sovereign, either, neither, atheism, deify, cuneiform, reinforce, albeit, Eid, Heidi, codeine), it becomes pretty apparent that this is one of those rules where there are a good few exceptions.

Furthermore, the glib little poem chanted jauntily as incontrovertible wisdom by teachers across the land is actually only half of the story. We tend to dispense "'i' before 'e', except after 'c'" as if it were a kernel of gospel when, in fact, it's only half the rhyme. The real rhyme has an added line, and is, "'i' before 'e', except after 'c', and when it sounds like 'a'". Things get perverted with age. I know this. I am old.

As regards rules, there is one that works, and works beautifully. To bowdlerise David Crystal, who is God-like at this stuff, and in whose elegant writing I first encountered this, there is a rule that all teachers need to know, but few do. This rule was first coined by a gent with the name of Ormin, which translates from Norse, as worm-man. Ormin was the very first spelling reformer, and so committed was he to his reformatory zeal that he went so far as to write a poem about spelling, 'Orm's Orrmulum', which came in at a princely 19,000 words long. It's not a hugely engaging read, but in it he created an orthography that used doubled consonants to show that the vowel was short.

---

5   Department for Children, Schools and Families, *Support for Spelling. The National Strategies: Primary* (London: DCSF, 2010), p. 106.

To understand this stuff, we're briefly going to have to divert into long and short vowels. This is fairly easy stuff, but is well worth anyone with any responsibility for literacy (i.e. anyone reading this book who spends any time with children) knowing. Basically, a long vowel is where the vowel says its own name: 'a' is said as 'ai', 'e' as 'ee', etc. A short vowel is where they make the sound we might usually tend to attribute to them:

a – 'ah'

e – 'eh'

i – a spiky 'ee'; 'ih'

o – 'o (silent 'c') h'

u – 'uh'

y – the long vowel 'e' is the sound for the short vowel 'y'. Confused? Me too. It's explained in the footnote.[6]

A double consonant – 'bb', 'cc', dd', etc. – signifies that the vowel sound before it is a short vowel sound. And I can't think of too many examples of where this doesn't work, so won't go to the bother of even attempting to correct a dead Viking who once thought it might be a nice idea to spend the long and very, very cold winter evenings reconstructing English spelling. But, if you are struggling to understand this, then here's a worksheet that you can use not only with your students, but which is worth doing yourself first to get the point. In proper constructivist form, I have given the answers as questions.

---

6   A note on 'y'. He's mainly a vowel. People tend to think he's mainly a consonant, or that he's one or the other, but it's not so. A 'y' is a consonant when he is at the beginning of the word and a vowel when he is elsewhere (in the middle or at the end). Think of how many words you know that begin with 'y'. We reach for 'yacht', then have to think a bit before we get 'yam'. It's mainly a vowel.

Worksheet with spelling activity – short vowels/double consonants CLOZE(ish) procedure

Go through the following piece of text and, using the clues in the footnotes if necessary, enter the appropriate word in the blank spaces. Crucially, however, you must say the word out loud as you enter it, noting the fact that it is a short vowel sound in all but one instance.

We were profoundly up the shit creek without a p____[7] negotiating the rocks and the r____[8] in the c_____[9] avoiding the t_____[10] of all the other boats. We s_____,[11] turned on the travel k____[12] and drank a cup of c____.[13] Wendy was l____[14] ch____[15], though still somewhat a_____[16] in her b____[17] hat. "What h_____[18] this evening?" she asked. "You o_____[19] me the chance to go boating, or to the b____.[20] I am sure I chose the l____.[21] Am I to a____[22] you lost the a_____[23], you a_____[24] m____."[25] Someone was clearly in need of a big c____.[26]

---

7   Implement for rowing a boat
8   What's left after something of wreck. Often in rock form.
9   Thin body of water.
10 Cyclists don't like this.
11 Came to a halt.
12 Implement with which one might boil water.
13 Muddy brown liquid. Awful without sugar.
14 Another word (the gerund) for the act of seeing.
15 A less noxious, though still demeaning way of referring to someone who is mildly overweight.
16 Erotic sounding word for seductive and attractive.
17 Much worn by farmers and seven-year-olds.
18 Occurred.
19 Presenting for acceptance or rejection.
20 Art form impenetrable to the working class male.
21 Definitely not the former.
22 Making an 'ass' of 'u' and 'me'.
23 Postal signifier of where you live.
24 Rubbish.
25 Horrid wriggly white worm that becomes a fly.
26 What you give someone when they are upset.

Taken from *Literacy* © Phil Beadle, 2015

The last of Cynthia and Robin's spelling myths are, "You can happily disguise misspelling with messy handwriting", that "You'll put students off if you correct their spelling" and, finally, that "Spelling isn't important. It's the ideas that count." On the first of these I would only add, well, that's certainly what a lot of my students have believed. On the second, I feed in that it is this kind of sloppy, unevidenced thinking that allows kids to carry on with the same misspellings through the space of a thirteen year academic career that has left some of them barely literate, and that there is no point in the English teacher taking a principled stand on the correct spelling of 'separate' when all the student's other teachers leave that same spelling uncorrected. It is the final point, though, which is where we came in, that brings us back to dyslexia.

DOES DYSLEXIA EXIST?

Before the filming of the adult literacy TV programme, I was in possession of some pretty unpleasant stereotypes that I am now ashamed of: middle class for thick etc. In my first Year 7 class, there were four children who were completely illiterate. They could not read at all. They were classed as being profoundly dyslexic, and the prognosis was pessimistic. Then they met one of my teaching heroes, Barrie McLennon, who has taught more kids to read in the poorest part of the East End of London than anyone else. I now correspond with all of these students on Facebook. The problem they had was not dyslexia, it was something else: they had just not met Barrie McLennon yet. A senior, very well-known educator once told me something about dyslexia that I shall report to you in the form of the drama-script in which it was originally presented to me:

Senior, Very Well-Known Educator: Of course, the problem with dyslexia is that it's often confused with two other conditions.

Me:	What are they? Oo! Oo! Tell me! Tell me!
Senior, Very Well-Known Educator:	The first is ABT.
Me:	Gosh. Never heard of it.
Senior, Very Well-Known Educator:	And the second is Instructional Dysfunction.
Me:	What's that?
Senior, Very Well-Known Educator:	Crap teaching.
Me:	And what's ABT?
Senior, Very Well-Known Educator:	Ain't. Been. Taught.

This is the view of a real expert in teaching children to read. And it is a view that I agree with, because I wouldn't disagree with someone who knows more than anyone else on the subject.

Dyslexia is real. No one really knows what causes it; though we guess that it's a wiring problem in the way the brain passes messages between the two sides. Do people have reading specific learning disabilities? Yes. Do people who can read perfectly well have spelling specific disabilities? Yes. Are there people unable to read at all because their brain won't let them? Yes. Does everyone who claims to have dyslexia actually have it? Hell no!

The serious and difficult issues that individuals with a reading specific learning disability have to grapple with as well as their guts, their coping strategies and the brutal stigma they must endure are all immeasurably cheapened, insulted and made as if nothing by the number of people who claim to have the condition who DO NOT HAVE IT. It is not middle class for thick, unless used as a badge of mild damage by idiots to claim either attention or some special dispensation for not trying very hard. To a certain extent their claims are an attempt at empathy: "I know how you feel. I am mildly dyslexic myself. I am at one with your pain." But, in truth, it always comes across like Russia planting their flag in a part of the Ukraine that is not theirs.

This is further compounded by the point that our friend, the senior, very well-known educator, makes above: that many of the young people who have been forced to carry around this badge were just not taught very well. There is also a problem that Ros Wilson raises about the bus only stopping at one stop. The Learning to Read bus arrives in the reception year, and again in Year 1. But what if you were not ready to get on the bus then? Well, tough luck kiddo. That's when the bus has been scheduled to call at this stop. If you weren't ready to get on it at that point, through no fault of your own, because of either your background or your wiring, then it's your fault: it doesn't stop there again. You've missed it, mate.

While we are on dyslexia, I'll add something I have noticed and a technique that I've had a bit of success with for helping those kids who struggle to spell. One thing I have observed throughout my career – and this is anecdotal, as I do not have a sample size big enough for it to be worth pursuing, and know nothing about research techniques – is that students who struggle with spellings often can't 'see' the word.

Here are three pictures:

Picture the spellings of these words in your head. Can you do it? Many of us have something approaching a photographic memory regarding spelling, and can just either hear the word, or see a picture of it, and straightaway see it in front of us (or up and to the right in my case) in our mind's eye. Kids who struggle with spelling do not have this faculty. For them, you say the word 'fox', asking whether they can see a picture of the spelling in their head, and guess what they see? A picture of a fox. This bears some relation to Paivio's dual coding theory,[27] but, y'know, who cares? What matters is that there are loads of kids for whom spelling is difficult, and this will affect the way that people see them as they pass through life, causing others to think they are somehow mentally deficient, as if you can't spell, people (often wrongly) assume other intellectual issues. What can we do here?

There's an idea that I've used, with some small success, with kids for whom it is a real struggle, and the idea is that you use imagery to learn spellings. According to Paivio, "Imagery is centrally important in facilitating long-term retention."[28] And this leads us towards the work of Bull and Wittock, who experimented with three separate classes of kids and a set of eighteen nouns.[29] They set up an experiment in which they would use different methods to teach the kids the definition/meaning of those nouns. One class had to create what is described as "self-generated imagery", another had "given imagery" and a further class just had the verbal definitions.

The verbal definition group, or control group, was told to learn each definition by reading the words and writing them down repeatedly during the

---

27 An emeritus professor of psychology at the University of Western Ontario who's still kicking (at the time of writing) at the age of 89. He came up with dual coding theory, which suggests that we have two distinct (though correlated) systems for encoding, retaining and retracting knowledge: the visual and the verbal.

28 Allan Paivio, *Imagery and Verbal Processes* (New York: Holt, Rinehart, and Winston, 1971), p. 327.

29 Britta L. Bull and Merl C. Wittock, 'Imagery in the Learning of Verbal Definitions', *British Journal of Educational Psychology* 43(3) (1973): 289–293.

allotted interval. The "given imagery" group received words, definitions and illustrations. They were instructed to read the word and definition and then write it down, once, and then to trace its picture. The instructions given to the "self-generated imagery" group were to follow the directions given to the second group, but instead of tracing the given illustration they were to draw a pictorial representation of the word and its definitions.

It was found, after due respect to statistical cautions, that the retention rate was better when 10-year-old children "discovered and drew idiosyncratic images to represent nouns and their verbal definitions".

As I said, I've had some success with a related idea: using self-generated imagery to remember not only the definitions of words but also the spellings. Here are three words you may not have heard of: autotonsorialist, dactylion and nidorosity; none of which, surprisingly, the spellcheck even attempts to recognise. They mean, in order: someone who cuts their own hair, the tip of your index finger and the sensation or taste you get when you belch raw meat. Do a trial on yourself, then trial it on two classes: one with just the words and one with self-generated imagery. These are not easy words to spell. See if the following template helps the kids to learn them. If it does, you have a new method to teach spellings for the kids who really struggle. It only really works with nouns.

Draw an image in the appropriate box to go with the spelling of the noun.

Autotonsorialist:	
Dactylion:	
Nidorosity:	

OTHER SPELLING STRATEGIES – CHUNKING

On the adult literacy TV programme there was nice young man who I didn't do as well as I would have liked with. I could not teach him to read. I was not good enough and I failed him. Channel 4, of course, gave not a toss about this when filming was over, but during the time the cameras were rolling their groundless pockets and sphere of influence were readily available (should there ever be a moment when someone transforms from chrysalis to moth, it would be professionally remiss of them not to have it on celluloid). During this period they were interested in this nice young man and his desperate need, and brought in a series of what they called 'dyslexia experts' to lay some coloured film over what he was reading and to patronise him. This had the effect of him nearly smacking one of them in the mouth, which caused me to realise that, in the vast majority of cases, there is a picture of a 'dyslexia expert' – it's an industry, baby! – when you look in the dictionary in search of a definition for the word 'oxymoron'.

However, Cynthia Klein was, and is, in a different league. On our first meeting she laid a word out – let's pretend it was the word 'Connecticut' – before me and asked me what words I could spot within that word. "Con, on, tic, I and cut," I replied, desperate to show I was clever enough to do this. She then did something that appeared deliberately designed to weird me out.

"How do you like it?" Cynthia asked.

"Huh?"

"How do you like it? Do you like it like this? Or do you like it like that?"

Cynthia was asking me how I wanted to chunk the word. Did I like it like this? Con-nect-i-cut. Or did I like it like this? Con-necti-cut. Perhaps I liked it like this? Co-nn-ect-i-cut. How did I, personally, like it? What was my preference?

This process is called 'chunking it down' and is followed by deliberate mispronunciation. You say the chunked down syllables a few times (perhaps while touching the paper which might have been cut up, or might have pen lines struck through where the preferences for chunking have been indicated), deliberately pronouncing them in chunks. To give you a few examples of how this works, say the next three lines out loud:

Gov-ern-ment

Par-li-a-ment

Mis-chiev-ous

This process may well embed spellings in your head, particularly those that are often said rather differently to how they are written. The practical issue with this technique (whether you are using scissors or a pen to chunk) is that the process of chunking down is so damnably exciting that people forget to do the first stage. The stages go like this:

1   Spot the words within words.

2   Chunk 'em down.

3   Deliberately mispronounce.

And they go in that order. Don't just jump to chunking because you fancy it.

ERROR ANALYSIS

The final, and potentially most useful, of Klein and Millar's ideas is error analysis. Spelling errors generally come in one of the five categories which they identify as follows:[30]

---

30   Klein and Millar, *Unscrambling Spelling*, p. 31.

1   Spelling it like it sounds (logical phonological alternatives).

2   Not knowing the rules (rule orientated errors).

3   Putting the letters out of order (visual sequencing errors).

4   Mixing up the sounds (auditory perception errors).

5   Missing out or adding bits (motor integration problems).[31]

It's always best to find out by doing things, so I'd like you to first read this charming piece of text, which is an actual real student's work that I found on the internet while looking for jokes.

Sticker Story – Hores

I like hores. Hores have other hores frinds. Hores like carots. You woudn't think they coud but they can put thir legs strait up. Hores make you feel good. My Dad wants a hores but my Mum says no. When I am 16 or 20 I will buy my own hores.

One imagines the writer is male, and that the Mum is right to keep such a tight leash on his Dad.

Your next step is to categorise the spelling errors this little charmer has made according to the criteria outlined by Klein and Millar. First, you write out the correct spelling in the left hand column, then write the spelling evident in the text and, finally, you tick the appropriate column for the error. If the student is spelling it like it sounds, tick column 1; if he doesn't appear to know the rules, tick column 2; if the letters are out of order, tick 3; if the

---

31   The bits in the brackets feel a little out of date and, to avoid confusion, I'd stick with the error category outside the brackets.

sounds are mixed up, tick 4; and if letters have been missed out, or even added, tick 5.

Correct spelling	Spelling attempt	1	2	3	4	5

You now have an assessment record of what this particular student's issue is and can identify the correct intervention. In this case, the poor, sweet thing keeps missing letters out. The beauty of this device is that you can tailor interventions so that they actually hit the student's specific learning needs, and you don't waste loads of time on generic approaches that they already know. Use it. It works.

THE DOLCH LIST/MOST COMMON WORDS

I have a candidate for the most boring book ever written: *The Dolch List Explained*.[32] It sits in my bookcase to the left of the half-broken manual typewriter I am typing this on, and I will never sell it, as it is a reminder to myself that dedication can lead to insanity. No person with the slightest grasp of the concept of balance would own a copy of this book. I not only have it, but have read it and even partially enjoyed bits of it.

---

32 Denise Eide, *The Dolch List Explained: Sounding Out the Sight Words* (Minneapolis: Pedia Learning Inc., 2013).

To explain, Edward Dolch was a pinch-faced feller who, in 1948, produced a book called *Problems in Reading* which contained a list of high frequency words, many of which cannot be sounded out (some can), which he had constructed some twelve years previously.[33] This list is 220 words long, is still used in the American education system and has led many people with rather too little in the way of a social life to valorise Mr Dolch as the father of sight words. (As opposed to hear words, feel words, speak words or smell words. What else could they be when you are referring to reading? It's like having a dinner that is advertised as being 'pan fried'. What else is it going to be fried in? A curtain?)

However, while the list – mystifyingly – is still used in educational institutions, and is still regarded as useful, it isn't actually the list of the most commonly used words in the written language. I've gone to a lot of tedious trouble to put the two lists together, and so would like you to have a look at them and see if you notice anything weird. This table features two separate lists of the 100 most high frequency words juxtaposed. I've given you some questions to help you.

- Go through the second column of twenty-five words. Are any of these regularly misspelt in your experience? What do you notice about the frequency of 'there' and 'their' in the most common words list?

- There are several italicised words in the Dolch list (eight in total). Find them. What do they suggest about the process that Dr Dolch went through to compile the list? (As a clue, the words 'Santa' and 'Kitty' feature in the full list of 220 words.)

---

33   Edward W. Dolch, *Problems in Reading* (Champaign, IL: Garrard Press, 1948).

Dolch	Most common	Dolch	Most common	Dolch	Most common	Dolch	Most common
1. the	1. the	26. look	26. they	51. get	51. when	76. ride	76. come
2. to	2. be	27. is	27. we	52. them	52. make	77. into	77. its
3. and	3. to	28. her	28. say	53. like	53. can	78. just	78. over
4. he	4. of	29. there	29. her	54. one	54. like	79. *blue*	79. think
5. a	5. and	30. some	30. she	55. this	55. time	80. *red*	80. also
6. I	6. a	31. out	31. or	56. my	56. no	81. from	81. back
7. you	7. in	32. as	32. an	57. would	57. just	82. good	82. after
8. it	8. that	33. be	33. will	58. me	58. him	83. any	83. use
9. of	9. have	34. have	34. my	59. will	59. know	84. about	84. two
10. in	10. I	35. go	35. one	60. yes	60. take	85. around	85. how
11. was	11. it	36. we	36. all	61. big	61. people	86. want	86. our
12. said	12. for	37. am	37. would	62. went	62. into	87. don't	87. work
13. his	13. not	38. then	38. *there*	63. are	63. year	88. how	88. first

Dolch	Most common	Dolch	Most common	Dolch	Most common	Dolch	Most common
14. that	14. on	39. *little*	39. *their*	64. come	64. your	89. know	89. well
15. she	15. with	40. down	40. what	65. if	65. good	90. right	90. way
16. for	16. he	41. do	41. so	66. now	66. some	91. put	91. even
17. on	17. as	42. can	42. up	67. long	67. could	92. too	92. new
18. they	18. you	43. could	43. out	68. no	68. them	93. got	93. want
19. but	19. do	44. when	44. if	69. came	69. see	94. take	94. because
20. had	20. at	45. did	45. about	70. ask	70. other	95. where	95. any
21. at	21. this	46. what	46. who	71. very	71. than	96. every	96. these
22. him	22. but	47. so	47. get	72. an	72. then	97. *pretty*	97. give
23. with	23. his	48. see	48. which	73. over	73. now	98. *jump*	98. day
24. up	24. by	49. not	49. go	74. your	74. look	99. *green*	99. most
25. all	25. from	50. were	50. me	75. its	75. only	100. four	100. us

We'll look at these in reverse order for structural purposes. The intriguing thing about the Dolch list (which, I remind you, is still given to American kids to memorise) is that there are some words on it that do not appear on the real list of the most common words: colours, pretty, jump and little. If these seem a bit twee it's because Edward Dolch's process was to read loads of kids' picture books and use these as a source of the most common words!

In both lists you will note that the words 'there' and 'their' are used in the language (and in kids' picture books) with more or less exactly the same frequency. And this leads us on to a nigh on unresolvable issue.

THERE, THEIR AND THEY'RE

There is not a single secondary English teacher or primary teacher who is not heartily bored – to the point of being prepared to eat their own tongue if someone could guarantee that they'd never have to correct the confusion of these words again – with correcting the endless misspelling of, in particular, the first two words in this heading. We have all more or less decided that there's no point with the other one, as there is no way they'll ever understand. It's not as if differentiating between these two words is at all in the realms of difficult; people understand quantum physics, for God's sake. But it seems that for some lazy eedjets, the sheer weight of brutal physical and pointed intellectual effort involved in so differentiating is not worth it, so they don't bother. Dealing with the disordered spellings of these two words is the literacy teacher's idea of fiercely head-butting a wall made of reinforced concrete, festooned with rusting nails, and expecting the wall to give way before your skull is panned in.

I am of little use here, I'm afraid. But there are a couple of principles that might help. The first of these is to practise a studied intolerance of sin. In most aspects of teaching, it is best to be the embodiment of the behaviour you want the young people to demonstrate themselves, and so, in general classroom matters, tolerance and a studied positivity is the way to go. With one major exception: if you are tolerant of the there/their/they're literacy crime, then they will be coming for your family next. There is no excuse for a 5-year-old, 11-year-old or 16-year-old to labour under the misapprehension that this rank idiocy is a minor and entirely forgivable slip; and any teacher who allows their students to mix up 'there' and 'their', thinking it is only a venal sin, is not worth their pay packet.

First, get your retaliation in early on this one. Cement the sin. Call them on it. Make it the first thing you teach every lesson for a week. Explain that the world will think they're idiots if they cannot get this right, and that the world will, in this instance, be entirely right. Explain that they will not be employable as anything other than a cleaner or a teacher if they continue to commit this error. Practise extreme prejudice, as if you don't, this error will slip into their lexicon of acceptable behaviours and will damn them to lives of misery and loss.

Second, point out that it is not actually just a sweet and humble spelling error. Point out that they are putting entirely the wrong word in the space, and that they may as well have used the word 'table' or 'cat' for all the sense it makes. Use this example:

They were looking after there ball.

They were looking after cat ball.

They were looking after table ball.

Do they make any sense at all? No, they don't.

Their was a shining light somewhere over their.

Cat was a shining light somewhere over cat.

Table was a shining light somewhere over table.

Cat was a shining light somewhere over table.

Table was a shining light somewhere over cat.

Gibberish. Total gibberish. Now stop doing it.

If we go back to the list of most commonly used words, it is undeniably interesting, if you are a literacy nerd that is, that the two words are juxtaposed in terms of how often they are used, and this is perhaps part of the problem. Michael Rosen once made an interesting point about this issue: he suggested that perhaps the problem is that, in schools, these words are always lumped together, and this actually helps to cause the confusion. Certainly, I've lost count of the number of classrooms I've been in that feature a large, purchased poster, framed in red, which lists the meanings of the three different words, and which is routinely ignored by every child in the room. There might be an argument to make use of this poster (you know the one) as a teaching aid, by cutting it up in front of the children and sticking the definition for 'there' on one side of the room, and the definition for 'their' deliberately and pointedly on the other. Whatever you decide to do about this issue, and I'd be intrigued if you'd found something that worked for you, don't give up. It is in giving up that we hand the car keys over to Satan, and sit in acquiescence as he drives us directly into a brick wall.

MEMORIES NOW ERASE MAN'S OLDEST NEMESIS, INSUFFICIENT CEREBRAL STORAGE

This is one of several available mnemonics for mnemonics. These can be useful to learn spellings of specific words, but implementing their use in class can feel a little like you are Michael Gove's dream made flesh, and that we are in the 1950s again, and everything is fine, and everyone knows their place, and the correct order of things has been correctly implemented. But if they work, they work. Mnemonics split down into those that remind you of the sequence of letters in 'difficult to spell words', and first letter mnemonics, such as the one above for mnemonics.

Here is a quiz that foxes most teachers I have given it to. The sequence of letter conundrums are a little cryptic on first sight: you have to find a word that goes in the gap, that makes sense contextually and to which the other words in the conundrum are a clue to the sequence of letters in that word. Alternatively, if you are still scratching your head, look up the answer to the first one (turn to page 154) and you'll understand what is required.

Sequence of letters

1   Do not _____ a lie.

2   A _____ must keep a secret.

3   The _____ is your pal.

4   There is an ache in every _____.

5   Be sure of your _____ before you start work.

6   A _____ is always there when the end comes.

7   The CIA have _____ agents.

8   Always smell a rat when you spell _____.[34]

First letter mnemonics

1   Dashing In A Rush, Running Harder Or Else Accident!

2   A Rat In The House May Eat The Ice Cream.

3   Never Eat Crisps, Eat Salad Sandwiches, And Remain Young!

4   Big Elephants Can't Always Use Small Exits.

5   Trails Of My Old Red Rose Over Window.[35]

Of course, acres of classroom and farmyard fun are to be had getting the whole class to invent their own mnemonics. This is best done as a starter activity in response to the many misspellings you have noted that more or less everyone is making in their books. Get all the students to invent their own for, for instance, fiery, pastime and privilege, vote on the best two or three and display these in animated form.

---

34   1. Believe. 2. Secretary. 3. Principal. 4. Stomach, or interestingly, teacher (kind of profound and desolate and true, innit)? 5. Measurements. 6. Friend. 7. Special. 8. Separate.
35   1. Diarrhoea. 2. Arithmetic. 3. Necessary. 4. Because. 5. Tomorrow.

PSEUDOMNEMONICS FOR TELLING THE DIFFERENCE BETWEEN SIMILAR WORDS

It is little known that there are, on odd occasions, two different spellings of what initially appear to be the same word: practice, practise and licence, license.[36] Here we are in the drab world of nouns and verbs, boy.

Noun	Verb
Advice Might I give you a word of advice?	**Advise** The one thing I would advise.
Licence He was given licence to wander round the off-licence like a buffoon.	**License** I license you to wander round the offie like a buffoon.
Practice "Practice, protein, practice, protein."	**Practise** Mo Farah had been practising all day for his voiceover for the advert for Quorn (which he doesn't actually eat).

You might want to remember which is which through the pseudomnemonic of remembering that the 'n' of nouns comes before the 'v' of verbs in the

---

36 These are all homonyms (words that are alike in form). They break down into homographs (words that are spelled the same, e.g. pervert – a sexual deviant, or to divert) and homophones (words that are pronounced in the same way, e.g. carrot and carat).

alphabet, just as 'c' comes before 's', so the words with a 'c' relate to the 'n' of nouns (as they are the earlier in the alphabet) and the words with an 's' relate to the 'v' of verbs (as they are later). Alternatively, you might want to buy a gun from a bloke down the pub and shoot yourself in the head.

Not enough people tend know that a stationary order is one that never gets to the stationers, as it tends to stand rather still. Those who are in charge of the production of primary school newsletters, check this please, as when you send a newsletter to parents requesting that they ensure their children bring the appropriate stationary in their pack folders on Monday, it really weirds the educated ones out. They grapple with the request, and I can attest personally to a wasted Sunday evening with my wife trying to properly conceive what the appropriate version of stillness is, and how on earth we would fit such an abstract concept into our son's folder. The pseudomnemonic here is that 'stationery' includes 'er' and so does paper, and that 'stationary' contains 'ar' and so does 'car'. Which is a bit stupid, really, because cars move, don't they? Unless they're broken down. Or don't actually exist. And even then, they might, as they exist only in an abstract world, move abstractly.

The final bugbear that can be partially solved by pseudomnemonics is the complement/compliment conundrum. The crap pseudomnemonic here is that a complement adds something to make it **e**nough; a compliment puts you in the *lime*light. See what we did there?

AND FINALLY ... A WORD ON THE SPELLCHECK

One of the reasons it is well worth teaching kids how to spell is to protect them from the malign influence and pitiful crutch of Mr Spellcheck, which has had the same impact on spelling as the calculator has had on mental arithmetic. The "Yeh, I could work it out, probably, if I could be bothered, but honestly, your honour, I can't muster the enthusiasm, as the machine does it for me" issue. Personally, I've found that the calculator has destroyed that mouldering part of my brain that used to be able to solve fairly simple division or multiplication problems relatively easily with only the briefest of consideration. I haven't used that part of my brain for a long time as my computer does it for me, and, consequently, it has ossified, died and broken off.[37] I excuse myself this for a reason: the calculator is eminently reliable. I type in the sum correctly; the answer comes out straight, true and unarguably correct. This same degree of propriety does not apply to the spellcheck, which is substantially less than 100 per cent reliable. If it were a reliable witness, then CC, a classmate of Da King, who you met earlier on in the book, would not have come up with the following rather interesting first line of an essay: "I make the moist of my friendships."

CC was, sadly for him, not aware that this is one of the words that is so taboo that it is banned in mixed company (unless, of course, you are making reference to the particular qualities of a Victoria sponge). Neither was he remotely aware that he had made an absolute howler of an error. The reason he wasn't at all aware that it was an error, as he couldn't spell for toffee, was because he was totally and utterly spellcheck reliant. CC, like more or less all the 'intervention' students I have worked with, tends towards using the same technique with spelling. Since they all work on what goes by the technical term of 'shit school laptops', they only ever have access to an outmoded

---

37 Booze may have played a part in this also.

and cheap version of Microsoft Word, which, unless you are clever enough to disable it, highlights errors in spelling as they are made. The methodology of the recalcitrant student here is to right click on this word, and find the list of options presented for the correct spelling. Being a recipient of something less than an education, CC, like many 'less engaged' students before and after him, simply chose the first option. "How would I know, Sir? It seemed so plausible." And he has something of a point. How was he to know how to spell the word 'most'? He couldn't spell for toffee. If he had been taught a range of spelling strategies, he might not be so reliant on a faulty tool, but he hadn't. No one thought it was worth doing.

There is another issue with the spellcheck that may concern you if you live in parts of leafy Buckinghamshire. The fact that it frequently speaks American. I too have suffered paroxysms of rage to scribe the word realise, replete with a subtle, marginally erotic and faintly suggestive 's' sound, to have it automatically replaced by the vulgar, crass Americanism of the rasping 'z'. Realize? I ask you. A little research into this, however, and you'll come to the certain realisation that your prejudice on this issue is just that. If you consult the OED it states regarding this issue, "In this Dictionary the termination is uniformly written -ize." Ize is referred to as 'Oxford spelling'. And Oxford is good, right?[38]

---

38 Interestingly, if you look at *The Times* of London they are dead against the Oxford spelling. So here we are, again, in the realm of house style. If it feels good, do it.

TEACHERS' IRRATIONAL FEAR OF GRAMMAR AND LACK OF UNDERSTANDING THAT YOU REALLY DON'T NEED TO KNOW MUCH

In the olden days, when people were properly respectful of the class divide, and when the poor knew their place and doffed their caps to their betters as they passed; in a better time, when people read for pleasure, when the thwack of leather on willow could be heard on village greens, and when immigrants were seen as a punishable novelty, they did this rather arcane thing to 11-year-olds. They would sit them in a room with squeaky parquet flooring towards the end of their primary years and make them do a rather weird test that seemed mainly to check whether they had the ability to crack esoteric codes and sequences. The results of this test were then used to separate the children at this young age into two groups: (1) the clever children, who went to schools specially designed for them, and (2) the failures, who went to what were called 'fail schools'. This delicate sieving often seemed to divide the children down class based lines, so that the children of the mummies and daddies with well-paid jobs more often than not found themselves to be clever, and the children of the parents with poorly paid jobs more often than not found themselves to be labelled stupid.

(This may have been, at least partially, the result of the test including questions about what household servants did or who classical composers were. Anyway. Who cares? Not me. This stuff has all been long consigned to the past. You don't get schools for clever posh children, or stupid posh children, any more unless you pay for them.[1])

THE KING IS IN THE ALTOGETHER!

What is of interest here is the nomenclature of these 'pass' and 'fail' schools[2] from the olden days: the schools for the stupid children who would go on to labour for the clever ones were called 'secondary moderns' as, at that time, consigning 80 per cent of the population to the dustbin of indentured slavery was considered, somehow, quite the modish and progressive thing to do. The schools for the posh children had a special name, which the children of the fail schools would never be able to understand: they were called 'grammar schools'.

HONESTLY, HE'S NOT GOT A STITCH ON!

The schools for idiots eventually, in another exercise in irony, became called comprehensive schools, despite the fact that no clever children went there. Some of the children who attended the stupid schools grew up to be teachers, who, thankfully, generally only taught in the stupid children's schools when they qualified. And these teachers looked at the word 'grammar' and shuddered, as grammar was what the clever children did, and was something that was clearly not for the likes of them. They weren't taught it during their childhood, because it was too difficult for them, and so they spared their

---

1 Or unless you live in Cumbria, Lancashire, Liverpool, Trafford, Wirral, Calderdale, Kirklees, Lincolnshire, Birmingham, Stoke-on-Trent, Telford, Walsall, Southend, Buckinghamshire, Kent, Medway, Reading, Slough, Bournemouth, Devon, Gloucestershire, Plymouth, Poole, Torbay, Wiltshire, Barnet, Bexley, Bromley, Enfield, Kingston, Redbridge or Sutton. They've died out, you see.
2 This is what the children who attend them call them.

students this bother, as they wouldn't have understood it either. And had they gone to the bother of grappling with something too hard for them, it would have affected what is called their 'self-esteem'. And now those children are adults and teachers, they wince at the mention of the word 'grammar', as it is still too difficult, and the very word is a reminder of their own failures and their own stupidity.

AND YOU CAN SEE HIS WINKY AND EVERYTHING.

Their suspicion was further confirmed when a funny little man with lips that looked just like a fishy's, who had been given a very important job title which he used all the time to refer to himself, would go on the telly and argue for what are called 'standards'. One of the ways he would do this would be to talk about a mystical thing that only clever people could understand: gerunds.

AND IT APPEARS TO BE TAKING THE AIR LIKE AN ELEPHANT'S TRUNK ON HOLIDAY IN LANZAROTE.

The funny man, who had clearly been to the plastic surgeon after he became important, and who is now writing a book called *Everything I Know about Whipping*, talked about these things called gerunds. And when he talked about gerunds all the teachers cried, because they couldn't possibly know what a gerund was, or how they would teach it, when they were doing the thing that was called 'raising standards', because it was too hard for them.

HE'S STARK BOLLOCK NAKED! WHY CAN NO ONE SEE THIS?

And the funny little fish-lip man, whose wife told lies about how she fell in love with him because she saw him in Abercrombie & Fitch pyjamas, enjoyed saying the word gerund. Because the fact that the teachers did not know what it meant proved that he could make them work harder, because that's what you do to idiots. They can't add anything useful, so you turn them into slaves.

NO PYJAMAS AT ALL.

But some teachers did a little research and found out that, really and strewth, a gerund is just a word that can be both a noun and a verb, and ends in 'ing': beginning, ending. As in, "As he was beginning (verb) he noted that he would one day reach an ending (noun), but ending (verb) the paragraph he also noted that it was not far from the beginning (noun)." This is hardly an elite piece of knowledge beyond the likes of us. Like most grammatical knowledge, it is pretty easy to understand if it is explained, and furthermore, and most importantly, it isn't of any real relevance or necessity.

When I am running the training I run at not hugely competitive rates to teach rooms full of teachers this stuff, one of the questions I ask them is, "How much grammatical knowledge do you think you have to be in possession of to be an expert writer? Not just functional, not just good, not just really good, but expert enough to be paid for it?" In truth, this is just padding so that I can sit down while they talk about something, but recently I had a response from an interesting teacher, Fidelma, at Hounsdown School in Southampton. She had previously been a sub-editor for *The Guardian*, and her reply was salutary. "None," she said. "I've worked subbing the work of major national journalists, and there was never any evidence that they thought about these things." It may be that they had assimilated them to such a point that they had become automatic and therefore invisible even to the studied eye, but I take this teacher's point. You don't actually have to know much grammar at all to be an excellent writer, and you have to know even less to be able to teach kids how to write with a degree of competence.

What grammatical knowledge do you think you need to be able to teach writing? I'm glad you asked, as I have an answer for you: you need to know the parts of speech. And that is pretty much it.[3] Why do you need to know

---

3   Yes, I know that subject–verb agreement is a big issue with younger kids, but you are a complete dongler if you can't get this right, or work out, as a teacher, that you teach it with the aid of a little kinaesthetic rote. For more on this see pages 176–177.

these? Well, first, because they bounce up against the rules for punctuation to such an extent that you'll struggle without them. If you can't identify a coordinating conjunction, then you'll struggle with commas; equally, if you can't identify an adverbial start, then that comma usage is lost to you too. You also need to know them so that you have a shared language with the students with which you can drive improvements in writing, and with which they can analyse how decent writers use the different kinds of words to drive their writing.

STOP BEING AFRAID OF THINGS THAT HAVE NO POWER OVER YOU. LEARN THE PIFFLINGLY EASY BITS OF GRAMMAR THAT ARE NECESSARY TO WRITE WELL, THEN TEACH THEM TO THE KIDS

Parts of speech, otherwise known as word classes or word families, are really just a categorisation exercise. Within (or without) the bosom of a sentence, words only perform seven (maybe eight) different functions, and the parts of speech are just a way of putting a name on those functions. They are the mechanics, the meta-language of writing, and if you are ever going to analyse how writing works with any fluency or insight, then they are a toolkit that you need easy access to. What is singularly shocking is that, despite the fact that students have been taught these time and again in primary, they still cannot properly distinguish between them in Year 11, and so cannot analyse text to the level that will be necessary if they are to get an A*. They all know that an adjective is a describing word, but I've lost count of the number of times I've asked a set of Year 11s, "What is a noun?" only to be greeted with a sea of empty heads, as, internally, I ponder the following phrase, "Well, that's royally screwed then, isn't it? They want 'C' grades out of these in three weeks flat. Ulp!"

I fail to see why the education system has failed so pitifully here: some of this stuff is a little boring and would perhaps feel technical to the DT teacher or the maths specialist, but it's hardly dovetail joints or quadratic equations. In truth, English teachers are all such galloping flibbertigibbets (even the women) that we are far too besotted with spending rather more time than is necessary or at all productive poring over a short paragraph in which some minor French existentialist discusses the blueness of the colour blue to be bothered with learning anything useful; and so we're not actually very clever at all.[1] Our heavyweight technical stuff – grammar – is neither technical nor heavyweight. If it's easy enough for English teachers to understand, it should be a total breeze for anyone who can do long division without sticking their tongue out.

The seven (maybe eight) different kinds of words are: nouns, verbs, adjectives, adverbs, pronouns, conjunctions and prepositions (the eighth is determiners). And we'll use this chapter to point out why they should be learned and known by all teachers, how you might teach them in your lesson and what the benefits will be when both you and your class can identify an adverb. I have noticed, since Gove was in situ, that knowledge of this field in primary pupils has improved – my 10-year-old son can now recognise an adverb – and for this alone, we should conclude that Satan is not all bad.

---

1   Though, boy, are we good at shirts!

DETERMINERS

We'll start with the one that everyone leaves out, as it is the least interesting of an admittedly fairly bad lot. Here are some determiners:

- Articles – either the indefinite article: 'a' or 'an' (which is not sure which one is the real thing) or the definite: 'the' (which is certain which one it wants)

- Demonstratives – y'know, 'this' and 'that'

- Possessive adjectives – 'my', 'your' and 'their'

- Quantifiers – 'many', 'few' and 'several'

Of interest here is the fact that the Wikipedia entry on determiners was clearly written by me when pissed. If you run the examples of determiners together in sequence, it reads, "*The* girl is *a* student! I've lost *my* keys. *Some* folks get all *the* luck. *Which* book is *that*? I only had *thirty-seven* drinks. I'll take *this* one. *Both* windows were open." Which sounds uncannily like a confused monologue I might have entered into in my early thirties at about 10.30 p.m. on a Friday night in a teachers' pub in East Ham.

You might also note that, if you teach young people from Eastern Europe, many of these languages are a bit slack with the determiners.

"What is that Woytech?"

"It is penis."

"It is *my* penis."

"No. Is not, Mr Beadle. Is Woytech penis."

"What is it doing out in the classroom?"

"Penis is in classroom, because it likes it on table. But I will put it in trouser, as you are nice teacher."

They are not a great deal of fun, determiners, and there's not much to know about them that is of any value in terms of teaching kids to write, other than knowing they exist and what they are called. They are *the* words that sentences wouldn't work without, but which don't fit into *the* other categories, and about *which* no one cares.

NOUNS

Really, if you don't know this I would suggest you go back to your school and shoot your English teacher(s); you will be found not guilty.

Judge: Why did you shoot that devoted public servant?

You: They were an English teacher and they didn't even get as far as teaching me what a noun is.

Judge: Fair enough, really. Case dismissed.

Nouns are 'thing' words. Generally, if you can put the determiners 'a' or 'the' in front of them, then they're nouns. Provided they are not of the abstract variety (love, hate, madness, yearning, etc.), if you can see it then it's a noun. And there are loads in your classroom to refer to. The question, "What can you see in the classroom, or out of the window, Craig?" will elicit a series of nouns. "Oh look," you can say, "all these things are what is called nouns." "I see only oceans of boredom," Craig belches. "Also a noun," teacher mouths smugly.

So far, so utterly humdrum. Where it gets even more intellectually challenged is in the only piece of knowledge about them that is at all important in terms of how such minor and very easy pieces of grammatical knowledge might affect their written abilities: the fact there are two varieties, the common and the proper. A common noun is more, erm, common: it's a thing, not a name. A proper noun is a name and has a capital letter. I teach this through some rote learning cunningly disguised to make it appear that I am not, in fact, a fusty old traditionalist. I present kids, in groups of four, with the following poem, with gaps in it.

Common/proper nouns

A proper noun's a place or name;

A common noun's a thing:

Like ____, or ____, or _____,

_____, _____, _____, or _____.

I will read this out in a call and response style with the whole class:

Teacher: A proper noun's a place or name.

Class: A proper noun's a place or name.

Teacher: A common noun's a thing.

Class: A common noun's a thing.

This goes swimmingly, though it is always a good idea to pretend that they haven't done it very well, and get them to do it a few times, as the learning here is really in getting the first two lines lodged firmly in their heads. Then we throw in the curveball: where the gaps are, teacher does a raspberry!!!

Teacher: Like sprr.

169

Class:	Like sprr.
Teacher:	Or sprrrr.
Class:	Or sprrrr.
Teacher:	Or sprrrr, or sprr, sprr, sprr.
Class:	Or sprrrr, or sprr, sprr, sprr.
Teacher:	Sprr, sprr, sprr.
Class:	Sprr, sprr, sprr.
Teacher:	Or sprr.
Class:	Or sprr.

What happens here is that, on the first raspberry, the students come to the not unreasonable conclusion that teacher is a fruitcake, and you might encounter a tiny bit of resistance from raspberry averse students. But not much. In primary this works a treat. Enthusiasm for it dies away a little as students get older, and as the rhyme progresses. By the last raspberry, the rasping sounds lose their enthusiasm to such an extent that they tend to resemble the apologetic flap of utter resignation sounded by the postern blast of an 85-year-old.

After this, get them into groups of four and ask them to fill in the blanks. This appears easy to me, but it can take a while. The key here is to let them know there is an ABCB rhyme scheme (i.e. the last word must rhyme with 'thing'). Tell them that they must fill in the blanks only with common nouns. Once they have done it, they must then recite it in fours; and only if it scans is it acceptable.

Eventually, one might hope that they come up with something like this:

A proper noun's a place or name;

A common noun's a thing:

Like kite, or badge, or baseball bat,

Floor, ear, pencil, or ring.

You might want to do this with subject specific language if you are so inclined. Here is my DT version:

A proper noun's a place or name;

A common noun's a thing:

Like file, or rule, or G-clamp,

Saw, drill, T-square, or an object for chiselling.

If this seems a little childish and intellectually facile, that's because it is. The only knowledge we are interested in here is getting students to know, in the form of a readily recalled rhythmic form, that a proper noun's a place or name, and a common noun's a thing. From here, we begin to look at capitalisation, which is far more complicated than you would ever have thought.

Before we look at capitalisation, though, it is a fun activity to just shout out a series of nouns and have the students shout back to you if they are common or proper. It helps here if you are a football fan and do not support the same club as the majority of students. Let's imagine that this example is set in a school in Eastbourne:

Teacher: Ear'ole?

Class: Common!

Teacher: Table?

Class: Common!

Teacher: Brazil?

Class: Proper!

Teacher: Badge?

Class: Common!

Teacher: Book?

Class: Common!

Teacher: Crystal Palace?

Class: Proper!

Teacher: Yes, proper. Brighton and Hove Albion?

Class: Proper!

Teacher: Nah, common my sons.

Proper nouns and capitals

We all tend to think that we know everything there is to know about capital letters. But we don't. In the table below are fifteen different rules for capitalisation. One of them, to quote *Sesame Street*, does not belong here; one of them is a fake. See if you can locate the fake rule.

1	Members of national, political, racial, social, civic and athletic groups – Crystal Palace, Asians, anti-Semites, Tory scumbags, Haringey Council, Anti Academies Alliance

2	Words and abbreviations of specific names (but not the names of things that came from specific things but are now general types: here they mean things like French letters and italics) – Keynesian, LBC, SACRE
3	Family members (when used as proper names) – I had an embarrassing incident with Auntie that I couldn't tell the other aunties about. Mother would have been disturbed.
4	The major words in the titles of books, articles and songs (but not short prepositions or the articles 'the', 'a', or 'an', if they are not the first word of the title) – an Amazon reviewer described Beadle's *How to Teach* as "Rubbish".
5	The first word in a sentence that is a direct quote – "First, where 66% of UK adults stated that they would feel embarrassed to tell someone that they were bad at literacy related tasks, only 48% of people would feel the same about telling someone that they were bad at maths."[2]
6	Periods and events (but not century numbers) – Great Famine, Renaissance, Second World War, Spanish Inquisition, eighteenth century

---

2   Nick Tiley-Nunn, *How to Teach: Primary Maths* (Carmarthen: Crown House Publishing, 2014), p. 3.

7	The names of gods, along with other more minor figures in whichever of the great global clubs you choose to belong to; their holy books too – God (it's his name, after all), the Holy Virgin, Ganesh, the Lord. (But you don't capitalise the non-specific use of the word 'god'. As in, "All the gods were grumpy with the amount of money coming in.")
8	Titles preceding names, but not titles that follow names – Mayor Boris; Boris, mayor of London
9	The days of the week, the months of the year and holidays (but not the seasons used generally) – Christmas, November, Monday, winter, spring
10	The first letter of a sentence
11	Trademarks – Apple, Coca-Cola
12	Directions that are names (North, South, East, and West when used for a political or cultural entity, but not as directions). "Go north, young man. Hit the North."
13	All the subjects on the curriculum – Physics, Maths, English
14	The names of countries, nationalities and specific languages – Bahrain, Spanish, French, English
15	Proper nouns (the names of specific people, places, organisations and sometimes things)

Did you spot the odd one out? It was all the subjects on the curriculum. In fact, only the languages (Latin, English, French, Spanish, etc.) are capitalised. All subjects are equal, but some ... In truth, this was just a cunning ruse to get you to read through what would otherwise have been an impenetrably boring wad of text about dull rules. But what I would hope happens is that you realise that capitalisation is not quite the easy stuff for babies that you might have thought it was, and that you might tear this page out of the book and stick it up on your classroom wall, so that students come to a similar awareness. A warning though: if you are a secondary teacher and you decide to actually teach the students something they have never been taught before, which is useful and that they do not know, they will not thank you initially. Moreover, they will think you are treating them like babies and will complain bitterly to your boss about you.

VERBS

There's little here for teachers outside of the arena of English and literacy teaching that throws up either heat or much light. A verb is a word that signifies some form of action. As we saw earlier on, the only really interesting thing about them is that you can't have a sentence without one, because if you did, then nothing would happen in the sentence and there wouldn't really be any point in it existing, as it is the verb that – structurally, at least – causes things to occur.

To teach what verbs are, it is marginally worthwhile reading a whole load out to the class and get them to do some form of stultified mime along with your tired recitation. At the end of this, voilà, we have an understanding that verbs are action words.

Here is a script:

> A verb is a doing word. Can I have a stooge, please? Run on the spot. Walk on the spot. Breathe. Breathe. Eat. Think. Chew. Drum. Bite. Breed. Stand. Cluck. Flap. Sit. Turn. Catch. Shine. Shrink. Sing. Dance.

Freeze. Hit. Mow. Do … five press-ups. Rest. Breathe deeply. Stand.
Go … back to your seat.

But this is pretty basic knowledge. For English teachers, it can be a profitable exercise, certainly when you are teaching poetry, to get the students to underline all the verbs in a poem, and then to put those verbs into some tabular form, so that they may examine how the verb usage fluctuates over the space of the stanzas. But I can't see that this technique would give forth much light outside of the English classroom.

What does work well is when you combine verbs with pronouns and conjugate them accordingly with actions. In terms of teaching subject–verb agreement, which, so I am told by the few primary teachers I am allowed contact with without being arrested, is a real issue at their level of things, then rote, again, may well be the way to go, as the issue of working class kids conjugating verb forms in dialect when they write has a real impact on their attainment.

This is an unsophisticated response to a knotty and seemingly intractable, and arguably 'unteachable', issue, so I recommend an approach that might, a decade ago, have been termed 'kinaesthetic learning', but is probably now better termed what it actually is: rote with actions. You can do this with any verb that needs some knowledge embedded about it – stink, pooh and smell work particularly well with classes of sillies, but we are really just in the realms of sniggering about the existence of pooh here. The real dividends in terms of learning come with the past tense of 'to be', and the technique is really as simple as ascribing actions to the pronouns and doing it en classe. The actions are as follows:

SINGULAR

First person: I stink – (point at one's own chest with the right index finger).

Second person: You stink – (point directly at an individual with an accusatory look).[3]

Third person: He stinks – (point at a male individual without looking at him).

PLURAL

First person: We stink – (cuddle the room at a distance).

Second person: You stink – (address a group of people that you like whilst looking at them directly, wave your right hand in their general direction in an inclusive gesture that encompasses the immediate environs of all those you want to accuse of stinkiness).

Third person: They stink – (wave your right hand in the general direction of a group of people about whom you feel – for the moment, and in a spirit of silly fun – contemptuous. Do not look at them at this point. They stink!).

This is, of course, childish drivel, but the kids engage, and from this point you can start looking at the arguably vaguely interesting stuff about

---

3   Differentiation here: if you have a stinky kid in the class, DO NOT POINT AT THEM!

different narrators and how a first person narrative differs from a third person narrative.[4]

ADJECTIVES

This is the only one that not only has every child been taught at some point, but they all still remember. "Oh yes, Sir, no problem: an adjective is a describing word; and, no, I haven't the foggiest as to what this actually means, and nor could I identify one, but I can parrot out the definition on request, as it's always seemed to satisfy my teachers as a piece of heavyweight grammatical knowledge that the education system has equipped me with. But being in possession of this dull sentence, that I can rote out on request, as I am merely a factory output trained in Pavlovian call and response idiocies, has positively affected my education not a jot. An adjective is a describing word. What does that mean?"

It's a useless piece of knowledge. Unless you use it to do something useful with. An adjective is a word that describes a noun. It's not just a piece of grammar; it's a piece of bloodless, dull grammar. It's not enough to describe something as a table, as this is what is known commonly, in staffrooms the

---

4   From here you can also divert into tense:
     "Why should you not be writing in third person past tense?"
     "Because every other kid in the country is writing in this person and tense, and there is the vague possibility that the person reading it may be somewhat tired of reading generic, uninspiring rubbish."
     "Nice response. And why are we trying to write in the second person present tense?"
     "Because that means that the reader is the same person as the main character, and that as they are reading it, they are also carrying out the actions, and, also Sir, that this seems of the appropriate level of intellectual challenge for a fourth set in a failing inner city school, because the only reason we are failing is that our teachers don't expect us to be geniuses. And we could be, if only anyone asked a little more of us."

length and breadth of the country, by its proper technical term: 'crap writing'. "He sat at the table." "Poor – see me." Why not describe it as a 'godless table', or perhaps even as a 'satanic table'? Adjectives can go either before the noun or, if they are in that kind of mood, after it. It could well be an ugly pair of trousers, a pair of ugly trousers or a pair of trousers that were struggling temporarily with their own notions of physical attractiveness.

In terms of equipping kids with a marginally more sophisticated sense of what they can already parrot out, a nice English teacher trick is to go on an adjective hunt around the playground or the local community. Equip kids with a pen and a notebook and go out on a walk. Look at the detritus that gathers at the bottom of the chain link fence that separates the children from a frightening world during the day, and write down words that might describe it: scratchy, tired, broken. Once you've spent half an hour in the great outdoors, and have fed the kids some of your best lines, then you come back inside, the students choose their favourite three and then animate them with colouring pencils, so that the word 'scratchy' looks kind of, well, scratchy; so that the word 'tired' looks in need of a kip; and that 'broken' is not fixed. Their responses to this activity will surprise you, and you will get some really nice and imaginative display work out of it. It will also give the students a constant reminder to avoid the obvious, as well as a resource if they are struggling in a piece of writing to find a decent adjective – just nick one off the display.

A concept that I've used successfully with students in terms of promoting the use of intriguing non-standard adjectives involves bringing a naked Action Man into class (I've actually got one which is a David Tennant dolly). I give a few of the students an article of his clothing each and ask the class what they would call him. They reply, "Action Man." And I'll ask them, "Action Man: common or proper?" I follow this up with asking them what else they might call him. "Dolly!" "Dolly: common or proper?" They get it all wrong, but at least we're trying. I then ask them, once they have realised it is David

Tennant, or Doctor Who, what they notice about him. "He's naked!" they reply with glee.

We venture off here into a lengthy monologue about how, whatever you call him – Tennant, Action Man, dolly – he is a noun, and that, currently, he is a naked noun. Then riff into an explanation that a noun that is not clothed in adjectives is called 'a naked noun', and needs to be clothed. We then ask those holding the dolly's clothes to come up with two adjectives to describe those clothes (colours are banned, as students reach too readily for these as a first response) before they are allowed to dress dolly. You can do variations of this with Buckaroo!, Twister, etc. "I am putting a twisted, sadomasochistic piece of rope on the knackered, plastic donkey." "Well, personally, I am moving my crippled, withered arm onto the lively, sunny red circle." The point being that younger students start routinely using two interesting adjectives before each noun. There comes a time towards the end of Key Stage 4 that you have to remove this scaffolding, when they start to make adult decisions about how they want to communicate in their writing, but as a rule of thumb, two adjectives before each noun does enliven their work.

There's another technique here that works quite nicely to add a more random element to their writing and to ensure that they don't just reach blindly for the obvious: that is to use one adjective that is appropriate and one that isn't. If we use the desk I am currently writing on, we would probably describe it as a rectangular, wooden desk; which would be competent but uninteresting. If we direct our camera on to something else instead – the pint glass of water on the desk, perhaps – and nick an adjective that would apply better to that – how about translucent? – we now have a translucent, rectangular desk, which is vastly more interesting and also subtly jarring. This technique works and, again, is orientated around getting kids to make decisions about their writing from a full armoury of possibilities.

ADVERBS

These are underused in children's writing, so introduce an instruction that, just like clothing the naked noun with adjectives, they must also cover the modesty of naked verbs with adverbs. They make a huge difference in terms of the appearance of competence and the vividness of describing any action: 'he collapsed' is one thing, 'he collapsed spastically'[5] quite another.

Adverbs are usually how you do something, and are covered almost comprehensively in terms of their technical stuff in 'Comma rule number 4 – adverbial starts' (see page 53). There's other stuff worth knowing about them though. My wife works for *The Times* as a graphic artist, and has made several high order friends; a few low ones too. One of our favourite people is an utter gent, Robert, who used to work for the business section, and who also wrote leaders and obits. I have asked the advice of this class act in handsome trousers about adverbs, and on the subject of split infinitives (this is where the adverb goes after 'to' and before the verb) was given the following words of wisdom: "My dear boy," said Robert, billowing smoke from a choice cigar, which he had previously dipped into a fine claret. "It's utter nonsense. In Latin you cannot put an adverb between 'to' and the verb, as it's all one word. However ..." (a drizzle of claret drops onto his cravat) "generally one would put the adverb after the verb as it is simply more elegant. However, as a matter of style, if any of my journalistic colleagues insist on banning split infinitives then I am going to totally tell them off."

In terms of kids' writing, they must make their own decisions, of course, but it can be a useful thing to advise them that often you add the adverb to the verb by putting it after it, as it just flows a bit more nicely, and is, as Robert says, a little more elegant. You can put the adverb before the verb – and

---

5   Don't be offended. It's a useful adverb.

there are times when it is technically correct and even necessary to do so – but do so knowing that it has a slightly jarring rhythmic effect.

In terms of fun with adverbs, there are a couple of games that are a minor delight and have some learning benefit. One is to print off a whole series of 'ly' words and to get the class to moan in the manner of the adverb: softly, sweetly, sadly, silently, etc. A variant of this, which I would only play if you are safe in your place of work, have a relationship of trust with the kids and fancy a giggle, is getting them to mime having a pooh in the manner of the adverb. It's a scream watching a class full of 13-year-olds work out whether they can pooh sophisticatedly. You can also play adverb charades, where you take a child outside, assign them an adverb and then have the rest of the class give them instructions that they have to carry out in the manner of the adverb.

Where things get important with adverbs is with the conjunctive variety when they appear in the middle of a sentence. As part of the day I run on spelling, punctuation and grammar, I show a slide with a smooth looking silver fox with a well-tended beard who is staring confidently at the camera, half-empty beer bottle near his deliberately folded left arm, and mouthing the words, "I don't always use conjunctive adverbs. But when I do I separate the independent clauses with an adverb."

He's a suave looking dude etched with the patina of success, and if it's good enough for him, then it's good enough for Graeme in your class. The main conjunctive adverbs are outlined in tabular form on page 55, but for ease of reference here they are again: additionally, also, alternatively, although, besides, consequently, furthermore, hence, however, incidentally, indeed, instead, likewise, meanwhile, moreover, nevertheless, next, nonetheless, otherwise, plus, rather, similarly, since, so, still, then, therefore, thus, whereas. Put them at the front of a sentence and they have a comma after them; however, put them in the middle and they have a semicolon before and a comma after. This is pretty important technical stuff for young writers;

however, they are never taught it. On the subject of 'however' and 'therefore' you have to judge whether you are running two independent clauses together, or you might, however, just be using it as an embedded conjunctive adverb for rhythmic effect. Go with feel here as to whether the semicolon, or what Ros Wilson calls "the two comma trick", is appropriate.

PRONOUNS

There is nothing whatsoever that is even mildly interesting about pronouns, with the minor exception of the fact that the second person singular is the same word as for the second person plural (the latter used to be 'ye', but it changed over time). You can play a silly parlour game with them that involves two people, who must be of the opposite gender, conjugating the verb 'to be' as a script.

Female: I am.

Male: You are?

Female: He is.

Male: She is.

Female: We are.

Male: You are.

Female: They are.

I got this from the head teacher of a private school who came to see me speak once, and promptly withdrew his invite to present at his school. I've never used it myself as I don't see that there would be much learning, and to quote Newfoundland fishermen, it seems it would result in "a wet arse and no fish caught".[6] But looking at it again, I can see that if you are working with kids at a very low level, then basic knowledge could be drilled in through the use of this, and you could get a half entertaining starter out of it.

What kids do need to know about pronouns is the terms first, second and third person, so that they can identify the different kinds of narrative and avoid combining the third person with the past tense.

CONJUNCTIONS

We've looked at these already in the section on comma usage, and they are imperative if you want to get the third of the comma rules right. First, however, we'll look at one of the forms of usage that is thankfully dying out; another one of the Sister Dimpnah rules that is a load of rubbish, but at least has some founding logic to it. It has always been perceived to be a solecism[7] to start a sentence with a conjunction. And there's a reason for this: they are meant to be joining words: the plaster over the crack that shows where two clauses have been put together. As such, since they join things, people have quite reasonably concluded that you can't have the joining word at the beginning of a sentence because it isn't actually joining to anything before it. But modern usage has meant that this, as a hard and fast rule, has died out; principally, I think, because journos enjoy deliberately starting sentences with conjunctions in order to prove that they are so dandyish and such devil-may-care rebels who are in no way tied to their expensive private school education, in anything other than their bigotries about state

---

6   Margaret Atwood, 'Falling Short: Seven Writers Reflect on Failure', *The Guardian* (22 June 2013). Available at: http://www.theguardian.com/books/2013/jun/22/falling-short-writers-reflect-failure/.

7   This is the breaking of grammatical rules.

education, and they can break any damn rule that they want. Consequently, in my house at least, starting sentences with conjunctions is known as 'the journalist's affectation'; and it is a little known fact that when you pick up your NUJ card you are also handed a certificate of permission from Rupert Murdoch that you may start sentences with conjunctions, as you are now qualified to do so.

As regards whether you teach this rule, I have the generalised feel that you should, but give students the instruction that if they want to break it, then it should be done deliberately.

If we go back to the connectives/conjunctions conundrum, I remind you that the term 'connective' is a collective noun, which covers a variety of different types of words.

Connectives is a collective noun for:

- Coordinating conjunctions (FANBOYS)

- Subordinating conjunctions (otherwise known as subordinators) (e.g. whereas, although, though)

- Conjunctive adverbs (e.g. however, hence, nevertheless, therefore)

- Semicolons

We've already seen that if you have a conjunctive adverb in the middle of a sentence, and it's separating two independent clauses, you bung a semicolon before it. What is even less well known is that the semicolons themselves can be the connective. Who'd have thought? Take a fairly standard compound sentence with a comma before a coordinating conjunction:

> I haven't done any paid work over the summer, so the Châteauneuf-du-Pape is not on the agenda.

You can actually get rid of the 'so' and replace it with a semicolon.

> I haven't done any paid work over the summer; the Châteauneuf-du-Pape is not on the agenda.

This is a fairly advanced trick, but not so advanced that my 10-year-old can't understand it and, as usual, I'd recommend you don't second guess kids' abilities to understand what you teach them. Just teach them it, and if it doesn't stick teach them it in a variety of different ways until it does.

Interestingly, the fact that you can use a semicolon instead of a conjunction has led some teachers to believe that you can't have a connective after a semicolon. This is nonsense. Ask Julian Barnes; he's always at it. Here he is on how time interfaces with emotion; categorically proving the grammar check is a fool:

> Some emotions speed it up, others slow it down; occasionally, it seems to go missing.[8]

PREPOSITIONS

And, lastly, the one that no one ever remembers from school: the position words. There are two kinds of preposition – temporal (related to time) and spatial (related to space) – and a decent way of getting this stuff into the heads of your charges is to ask them to get in relation to their chair in the manner of a series of prepositions. The following script has been finessed over years, and I recommend it wholeheartedly to you:

---

8   Julian Barnes, *The Sense of an Ending* (London: Jonathan Cape, 2011), p. 3.

Teacher to shout out the following:

> Stand behind your chair. Sit by your chair. Get in your chair. Stand on •
> your chair. Go near someone else's chair. Walk past someone else's
> chair. Go up your chair. Lie along your chair. Get below your chair.
> Walk around your chair. Get inside your chair. Get onside your chair
> (you have to have one chair between you and the goalkeeper). Oh,
> never mind.

There are japes to be had in throwing in the odd temporal preposition in order to keep things ludic, to deliberately do the kids' heads in and to elicit the kind of abstract artistic thinking that some gap year students on Twitter would argue was a form of low expectation. Why be intellectually playful when you can just tell them things?

Once they've got the notion of a preposition, you have to look at whether you are allowed to put one at the end of a sentence or not. And we are going to look at this through the process of me telling you the second best joke in the world. The best joke in the world ends with the line, "It's funny, you don't look Jewish," but it would take too long and would be irrelevant, so I am now going to tell you a joke that I have told to reasonable sized audiences in the region of 100 times. It is a very good joke indeed. It's the second best joke in the world. No one has ever laughed at it. If you don't laugh at this joke it doesn't mean that the joke is rubbish; it means that you are rubbish. It is basically an IQ test. If you think this joke is funny, then you are clever enough to be a teacher; if you don't, pick up your P45 on the way out, and don't forget to slam the door.

Here is the joke:

David Beckham walks into a library.[9]

And it is a posh library in Kensington and Chelsea. He approaches the chief librarian who is sat behind a pristine oak desk, wearing a string of fake pearls, and is a right snooty mare.

"Oh!" she exclaims as David stands, innocent as a fawn, in front of her. "Mr Beckham! We weren't expecting to see you here."

"This is a library, isn't it?"

"Yes, Mr Beckham. It is a library."

"Oh great. Can I have cod and chips twice?"

So there it is, the second best joke of all time. You didn't laugh, did you? No one ever does. I feel completely wasted sometimes. It goes on …

"No, Mr Beckham. We do not sell cod and chips in a library. We lend books."

"No pickled egg, then?"

"No, Mr Beckham. No pickled egg."

"OK then, can I take a library book out?"

At this, the preposterous snob in a scratchy A-line skirt rises on spindly haunches and spits out with a venom that is entirely inappropriate for such a meek profession, "This is a library, Mr Beckham! And, what is more, it is Kensington and Chelsea Library. We never end sentences with prepositions! It is the kind of grammar up with which we cannot put!"

---

9   That is not the joke. But it is the only bit that people ever laugh at.

What could David have done to satisfy this lady? And let not our answers here wander towards contemplation of the profane.

Well, he could have pointed out that in this instance 'out' is not, in fact, a preposition, but is part of a phrasal verb (take out), but David's grammatical knowledge wasn't working to that level on the day in question. Alternatively, if he was going to take what the nasty lady said as gospel, he might have used the word please, or rearranged the sentence so that it read, "Can I take out a library book?" Alternatively, he might have appended the words, "You vile and ghastly pedant!" to the sentence, or he could have just waved his wad in her general direction.

Better than any of these, though, would have been to point out that there is no language anywhere that has ever had a rule that you don't end sentences with prepositions; that saying, "To whom are you talking?" rather than "Who are you talking to?" comes across as pompous; and that no one believes this any more as, in truth, these pieces of elite grammatical best practice are just a way of making ordinary people feel as if they are somehow stupid because they don't have access to Latinate constructions. But David didn't come up with any of these responses. He just looked sad, like he had been really badly told off, and skulked out, crying, never, ever, ever to try to confront his demons and pick up a book again.

So, the not ending sentences with prepositions is just a piece of ignorant snobbery that doesn't fit with how we use language. Steven Pinker points out that its invention can be traced back to the poet John Dryden trying to show off that he was a better writer than Ben Jonson (who, at that time, had already been dead for decades): "The prohibition against clause-final prepositions is considered a superstition even by the language mavens, and it persists only among know-it-alls who have never opened a dictionary or style manual to check."[10]

Having said that, getting kids to recite this rap is quite fun:

The Preposition/Proposition Rap

A simple preposition: it tells you your position,

Be it in relation to the time or to the ground.

It's a sho' nuff equation, which tells you your situation

To the objects that are below or are around.

Oh, but on the other hand, a proposition's not so grand:

It's not in above, below or roundabout.

Well, it sure ain't nuclear fission,

Don't end your phrase with a preposition

Unless, of course, you're asking someone out!

This works really nicely if you ask the kids to do it in twos, either rapping it simultaneously or doing a line each, tag style. It also helps if you play some suitably mid-paced hip hop in the background. A word of warning here though: check the track for obscenities first. I made the error once, during an observed lesson, of putting on a hip hop compilation that an aficionado friend of mine had given me, as a backing for this activity. I didn't look at the track listing before putting the song on, which it transpired was by a particularly unpleasant group of violent misogynists whose names I can't

---

10 Steven Pinker, '10 "Grammar Rules" It's OK to Break (Sometimes)', *The Guardian* (15 August 2014). Available at: http://www.theguardian.com/books/2014/aug/15/ steven-pinker-10-grammar-rules-break/.

recall. I'm not entirely certain the twin set and pearls external consultant was hugely impressed with the initial lines of the, erm, 'song' 'Bust a Nut', which would be unlikely to win a Nobel Prize, and which made references to a variety of practices female canines and garden implements might involve themselves in if they were heavily pressurised into doing so by someone with a gun; specifically, a form of showering that doesn't sound as if it would get you very clean. Didn't get an outstanding that time: "Mr Beadle requires improvement."

WHAT TO DO WITH THIS STUFF

Here are a couple of activities that I use as an English teacher, which probably won't have much use across the curriculum, but which are valuable to develop students' writing if you are responsible for this. So, sorry if you are a DT teacher. You can skip this bit.

Sentence kernels

I've been told this activity is called sentence kernels. To prep the kids for it, tell them that you are going to do something so incredible that they will barely believe their eyes, that is a bit dangerous; they are to write down what you do once you have done it. You have to ham it up a bit here. Let them know that you require complete silence for this, as it takes you a brief while to get into the particular headspace that this activity requires, but it will be worth the wait. You are about to do something that is unbelievably difficult, and they are going to have their minds blown completely!

Go to one side of the room, inhale deeply, psyche yourself up and walk to the other side of the room. That is it, and that is all! You walk to the other side of the room.

Perhaps on a first run-through they didn't fully grasp the awe inspiring significance of what you've shown them, so just this once, and only because you like them, you will do it again. They must write down what they see this time. And you do exactly the same thing again, only this time from the other side of the room.

Get the kids to share what they've written and they will come up with a mild variant on: "The teacher walked across the room." Inform them curtly that this is shoddy and unobservant work indeed, and briskly ask them to copy, yes copy, down the following table.

Adjective					
1.					
2.					
3.					
4.					
5.					

Then ask them to come up with five words to describe you (adjectives) that they must write in the left hand column.

Adjective				
1. Boring				
2. Smelly				
3. Ugly				
4. Mean				
5. Musical				

Careful of your ego here, as they are rarely complimentary, and if you are not steeled it can hurt quite a bit. They must then use the technique of describing something with a word that does not apply to it, and fill in the second column of adjectives with words that do not apply to you. Like so:

Adjective	Adjective			
1. Boring	Kind			
2. Smelly	Silly			
3. Ugly	Serious			
4. Mean	Funny			
5. Musical	Normal			

And then a line of nouns that could be used to name you with. Yes, you are a teacher, but what else are you?

Adjective	Adjective	Noun		
1. Boring	Kind	Idiot		
2. Smelly	Silly	Creep		
3. Ugly	Serious	Pervert		
4. Mean	Funny	Monkey		
5. Musical	Normal	Mockney		

Then a set of verbs. Yes, a character can 'walk' across a room, but look again, what am I really doing? At this point you do a zig-zaggy, drunken stumble across the room. And they write:

Adjective	Adjective	Noun	Verb	
1. Boring	Kind	Idiot	Skips	
2. Smelly	Silly	Creep	Paces	
3. Ugly	Serious	Pervert	Lollops	
4. Mean	Funny	Monkey	Stumbles	
5. Musical	Normal	Mockney	Dances	

And, finally, how was I doing it? Dance across the room again in a manner so free spirited that they might mistake it for joyousness, and get them to fill out the adverbs column.

Adjective	Adjective	Noun	Verb	Adverb
1. Boring	Kind	Idiot	Skips	Effeminately
2. Smelly	Silly	Creep	Paces	Majestically
3. Ugly	Serious	Pervert	Lollops	Comically
4. Mean	Funny	Monkey	Stumbles	Flightily
5. Musical	Normal	Mockney	Dances	Stupidly

The kids must then read across and choose their favourite line. Of the above I think, "The ugly, serious pervert lollops comically", would cause any reader to immediately involve themselves in the kind of questions a decent sentence should ask of you:

- Is the fact that he is ugly the reason he is a pervert?

- Why is the pervert serious? Is he serious about his intentions or serious about being a pervert? Is a pervert always a pervert, or does he get a day off now and again?

- Lolloping seems unperverted. Perhaps he *is* having a day off.

- His comic movements don't seem to match with his pervert status. Is he a comedy pervert like on the seaside postcards, or – oh, God no! – is this the ... walk ... he ... uses when he has just committed a vile and depraved act and has left his victim, bleeding, by the side of a road? Is this why he has a skip in his step? Is the writer playing the most horrific game with us, leading us to believe that it's all OK, when, in fact ...?

This is what real writing does to readers: it causes them to engage in an intellectual process to decode meaning and detect nuance of intention on the writer's part. "The teacher walked across the room" doesn't cause this process to happen. Consequently, I advise emerging writers to use some of the principles contained within this exercise when they are writing fiction:

- Two adjectives before each noun. Not always but often.

- Second adjective to be sourced from somewhere else.

- Don't choose the obvious noun. Try the fifth one you think of.

- Same with verbs.

- Affix an adverb to nigh on every verb. It doesn't even have to be a good one to work, but a good one's worth looking for.

Stick these on the wall.

If your students apply these rules, and you grind them in with lots of practice, lots of reminders and lots of target orientated diagnostic marking, their writing of fiction (and to a certain extent non-fiction) improves radically. I know this because I am really experienced and have improved the writing of hundreds of classes, and you should just trust me and try it.

Consequences

Another activity that works really well as a way of using grammar in an entertaining manner, and that also works quite nicely as an AfL task in which you are assessing the class' understanding of the terms, is related to a game you might have played as a child. By way of context, when I was growing up, our family were among the last in the street to acquire a colour telly, and my brother and I spent the long winter evenings avoiding *Tomorrow's World* on the black and white as Raymond Baxter's hair scared us.[11] We'd sit in the somewhat over glamorously named 'middle room' with reams of plain paper and a couple of 2H Staedtler pencils with stripes the colour of wasps. Dave (my brother) and I would both draw a weird alien head, fold a flap of paper over towards us so the drawing was obscured, then we'd pass it over to each other. We'd repeat the process by drawing a weird alien neck, always remembering to draw on the paper directly under the existing flap and that you should NEVER WRITE ON THE FLAP. This is cardinal. Then onwards and downwards we'd go drawing, in turn, a weird alien body, a weird alien pelvis, legs and feet. Eventually, the game would reach its glistening crescendo: we'd open up the pictures and we'd cry in unison, "Great. We've got two crap pictures. Dad! When can we have a colour telly?"

I believe middle class people play this game with actual words and call it 'consequences'. And since schools are institutions which superimpose middle class values on working class kids, whether they want them or can cope with them or not, we are going to do the same. But in doing so we are going to test the grammatical knowledge of our charges.

Here is the sequence:

1   Either the word 'A' or 'The' (the indefinite or definite article) followed, right next to it, by an adjective.

2   Fold, then swap.

3   A further adjective or adjective phrase.

---

11   Do not try thinking about this if you are under 40. Pass on. Nothing to see here.

4   Fold, then swap with someone else this time.

5   A common noun.

6   Fold, then swap with someone who is not on the same table as you.

7   Verb, third person, present tense. Ends in 's'.

8   Fold, then swap with someone who is not of the same ethnicity,[12] gender, religion, whatever as you.

9   Adverb.

10   Fold, then swap with someone whose shoes you dimly envy.

11   Preposition.

12   Fold, then swap with someone you haven't spoken to today.

13   Either the word 'a' or 'the' (the indefinite or definite article) followed, right next to it, by an adjective. But not the same as on the first line.

14   Fold, then swap with the person you most love in the class.

15   Common noun.

16   Swap with the person next to you.

17   Open them.

18   Laugh your socks off.

---

12 Don't balk at this. The kids prefer it if we are open about the fact that they are not all the same. Unless, of course, you teach in a mono-culture; in which case it won't really work, and you should consider coming and teaching where it counts.

There are eighteen steps to this activity, and since I invented it and have used it quite a bit, I have identified a few technical aspects that will help it go sweetly.

- We are not at home to big flaps in this game.

- DO NOT WRITE ON THE FLAP. WRITING ON THE FLAP WOULD BE A VERY, VERY, VERY BAD THING TO DO. HOW MANY VERYS? THREE VERYS. THAT'S ONE HELL OF A LOT OF VERYS. DO NOT WRITE ON THE FLAP.

- Keep your writing small. There are eighteen steps.

- Kids, it's really better if you don't swear. It's good that you are able to tell that these words are often fruity Anglo-Saxon adjectives, but it's much funnier if you avoid them.

The results you get out of this are beautiful. Here's a sample:

> The overly proud, preposterous ego jumps sophisticatedly beneath the purple cradle.

> A driven, delicate fox lives leeringly under a specific table.

> The collapsed, bilious tortoise belches sadly around the coloured nose.

Again, we are in the region of students reading these and the writing automatically inspiring them to involve themselves in some intriguing inferences. The random element of it also brings some unusually lovely accidental juxtapositions and clashes. Would a writer consciously create the collision of alliteration on 'driven' and 'delicate'? Perhaps. But would they have had the brass balls to follow this up with the further alliteration of 'lives leeringly'? Only if they were trying to show how very ambitious they were to create work that had a really quite developed sense of audience. And you truly feel for the tortoise; it sounds like he's been having a very hard time.

Of course, there's far more to grammar than this, but you don't really need to know it, unless you want to spend your declining years wasting time writing complaints to newspapers about dangling participles. Knowing the parts of speech and how they bounce up against punctuation is all you really must know if you are to write as fluently as you speak. And once you and your class have this shared knowledge, then you can start delving into the real work, which is orientated around the higher levels of manipulating your readers' responses, using humour and playing stupid games with the form. Once you know the parts of speech and the punctuation you can involve yourself in *jouissance*: the Barthesian idea of constructing writerly texts that explode the limits superimposed on them in terms of how you play, trans-gressively, with language to the point that one might experience a degree of narcissistic elation. (But not to a Lacanian extent, of course.) Alternatively, you can write a pretty good letter of complaint to the dole office when they've cut your benefits for no good reason.

NOT ENOUGH UNDERSTANDING OF WHY STUDENTS CAN BE RELUCTANT WRITERS

I spent three days in 2012 in a school in a grim Northern Town that has a rude word in the middle of its name. I had been asked to work with a group of young people who, it was said of them, "No one could do anything whatsoever with." As usual in these situations, you enter the room smiling, be nice to them and find that the young people concerned are perfectly nice themselves, and will work well when you create conditions in which they feel safe to do so. This particular group of young people were actually quite articulate when asked for their opinion as to what the issue really was, and why I had been told by professionals that they were, and this is an exact quote, "completely intractable".

"We're not lazy, Sir; and we hate it that our teachers are always telling us that we are. We've just never really achieved anything with writing since we were small, and we've got kind of locked. We're scared of it and the only strategy our teachers have for making us less scared of it is calling us lazy, and it doesn't work, Sir."

This is the gist of what they were saying. They were giving me a really privileged insight into the mind of the reluctant writer. Their lack of previous success in this field had caused them to have some form of emotional problem with writing as they associated it with failure. The solution here is pretty obvious: give them a taste of success.

Before we look at this in any detail, however, let's consider one of the specific problems that boys experience in constructing a written response, which is often the pen in their hand and, indeed, the hand itself. There's a section in boys' achievement expert Gary Wilson's book, *Breaking through Barriers to Boys' Achievement*, in which he lists the responses a set of Year 4 boys gave when they were asked the simple question, "Do you like writing?" They include the following:

"No, it hurts your arms."

"No. I'm rubbish because of my handwriting."

"No. My hand gets really sore."

"No, because of my hand hurting."

"Writing hurts my hand."[1]

This is a fairly definite and standard response. It hints at the enormous difficulties pen control sometimes presents young males, and the problems that extended writing activities can cause them physically. Foundation teachers have become hip to this, and now, before they ask very little boys to even try to pick up a pen and write with it, they ask them to do lots of cutting with scissors to develop the fine motor skills they will need. Go into any Year 11 English exam in May, where kids are having to write reams of irrelevant text analysing leaflets to guess the graphic designer's reasons for putting a picture where it is (when actually there was a template), and note who it is that is shaking their hands as if trying to get some water off them or are massaging their poor aching fingers. It bloody hurts doing huge amounts of extended writing.

---

1 Wilson, *Breaking through Barriers to Boys' Achievement*, p. 18.

GIVE THEM A TASTE OF SUCCESS

Go back to pages 113 and 114 and re-read the section on word counts. Then implement them. The issue with a young person, who you'll often find is a boy, who really struggles with the emotional baggage of continued perceived failure, can be confronted by scaffolding their responses with skilled task setting. Word counts work. They chunk down work into manageable pieces.

You can also take a more punitive approach to this, which also works. If you are in a class in the lesson before break, lunch or home time, and you have a student who is struggling to pick up their pen, give them the first sentence, so they no longer have the excuse that they can't start because they "Don't know what to write", then put a pen mark halfway down the book in the left hand margin, and inform them that they will be allowed to go to break, lunch or go home when they have reached that point in the book in their writing. Mean it. And enforce it.

But, ultimately, it is worth making writing worth doing by placing it within a dazzle camouflage so students enjoy it. One technique, again from Gary Wilson, that I've used lots of times to good effect is to present the students with what he refers to as a "guided visualization".[1] You put a picture on the interactive whiteboard, and then take them through a series of steps: "You are here in the picture, looking in this direction: describe what you can smell

---

1   Wilson, *Breaking through Barriers to Boys' Achievement*, pp. 26–27.

in the present tense, and you must use adverbs." Four or five steps works nicely, as does giving them only a minute to write each paragraph. This is a really useful first lesson technique, as you'll often find that those children for whom two lines of drivel is considered a decent fist of work for a lesson write absolutely loads, and you have called them on their protests that they "Can't think of anything to write" before they've even tried on the coat of this flimsy socialised excuse. You can use this technique in subjects other than English too. In a science lesson, show them a still of an experiment, place them in four different parts of the picture and ask them what they can see using the key words from the scheme of work. In history, examine the narrative of the Bayeux Tapestry from all sides of the picture or story. In MFL, construct the dialogue the couple in a Doisneau print are having at the moment just before they kiss.

One of the issues that students struggle with is varying their sentence lengths. It doesn't matter how many times you seem to tell them that a decent writer, who is in charge of the rhythm of the writing and who doesn't want to bore their readers, will write in a variety of sentence lengths, it never seems to get through. Oddly, I have an input here that stems from my days as a correspondence clerk in the shareholder relations department of the Abbey National from a quarter of a century ago.

The correspondence clerks were the ones writing to punters telling them that they weren't getting any free shares because they'd signed the form wrong when they opened the account, and we're very sorry and all that, but actually we're not, as we're just doing this to pay the rent, and actually care vastly less about Abbey National corporate policy than you do. I spent four years there, mainly informing an ex-army man that I wasn't getting my hair cut, because it was my hair, not his, and it wasn't as if it was growing into my brain and impairing my intellectual function, and that you didn't have to have short hair in order to write decent letters of apology. At the time, the Abbey were in the habit of trying to simplify their communications, as they were at the white heat of modernity and weren't at home to arcane formal English, baby.

So they brought all us poor correspondence clerks up into the boardroom to be lectured at by a half-wit with presentable hair who was certain of certain certainties. He represented a branch of the "intellectual wing of UKIP"[2] called the Plain English Campaign. It is not actually a campaign but a commercial training and editing organisation, which John Humphreys is a fan of, and which has been described thus by the writer Oliver Kamm: "The joke – not that it's funny – is that a body ostensibly concerned with clarity of language is both incompetent in its own use of English and heedless of the task it sets itself."[3]

The guy from the plain English Campaign had some interesting things to say about sentence length and introduced a concept he called 'the fog index' – a metaphor that I remember thinking, even then, had all the shining intellectual brilliance and charisma of a pair of grey Marks and Spencer's slacks – and that, "For every word you write in a sentence over twenty words, the fog gets denser."

"And you would be the walking embodiment of a seventy-five word long sentence," was what I didn't say.

He went on, "Thirteen words is the optimum sentence length for clear communication."

"Nope. I've got a two word long sentence that would communicate my thoughts with utter clarity," was also what I didn't say. Again.

I lasted another few weeks before deciding that the dole would be preferable.

---

2   Gill, 'Table Talk'.
3   Oliver Kamm, 'Plain English Baloney II' (24 March 2004). Available at: http://oliverkamm. typepad.com/blog/2004/03/plain_english_b.html/.

But the thoughts of idiot boy on sentence lengths hung around like the crushing smell of moral disappointment at an orgy. The majority of my classes seemed to think that a seventy-word long, completely unpunctuated sentence was a completely valid technique, so I decided that we'd do a bit of plain English in a school in the East End.

It transpires that kids being in possession of the knowledge that a twenty-word sentence is about as far as they want to go, unless they are experts in measuring out fascinating subclauses (and marking these off with an interesting and technically well-achieved variety of punctuation) is a really pretty useful piece of information. With this they can start self-assessing. "How long is this sentence? Sir says I shouldn't go over twenty words long, and this is thirty-five; he might forgive me if I use a semicolon at some point. Or should I shorten it? Is there a better place for the full stop?" This is potentially the realm of the flow chart, or even of the dry procedural that is lovingly stuck to the wall by the teacher who thinks it will solve everything, only for it to be resolutely ignored. I may write such a document one day, but today is not that day.

What I have noticed in the dizzying world of asking kids to write in different sentence lengths is that they completely ignore the marking.

Marking: Targets: 1. Please try to write in a variety of sentence lengths.

Student: I am a student; therefore, I shall ignore the piece of advice that Sir seems to so enjoy writing that he has written it at the bottom of my last seven pieces of work in the appropriate manner for my station. I shall ignore it studiously and with not a little rigour too.

It got to the stage that there was little hair left to tear out and, out of respect for the remaining few limp locks, I decided to obey the old Cockney aphorism, obedience to which that has served me so well in terms of dealing with teaching materials written by the daft or irredeemable, which is: "If you want something done well, do it yourself!" If you want the kids to write in a variety of sentence lengths, then do it for them.

The technique here, which I am aware I have written about before (but which is such a doozie it bears repetition), is to dictate the sentence lengths they will write in. Get a class to select, in their heads, two separate numbers: first, a short number between 1 and 5; second, a longer one between 6 and 20. They do so, and I go round the class requesting either their long or their short number. You can play with this, selecting only the responses that you think will lead to interesting patterns. As the kids don't know what they are selecting the numbers for, you can play on this ignorance for fun, answering that you really like the response when a number is suggested that fits into your scheme, and being dismissive – "Are you insane?" – when a number is suggested that doesn't fit with the way you want things. Broadly, you want a balance of long and short sentences and repetitive patterns in the smaller sentences. What happens when kids write to prescribed sentence lengths, and there are repetitive patterns of short sentences, is that their writing takes on the patina of what is called 'style'.

Here's the kind of numbers you might be looking for when asking for suggestions from the dull crowd:

3, 3, 3, 15, 17, 20, 1, 11, 8, 7, 20, 1, 2, 3, 15, 2, 2, 2

The briefest analysis of these numbers reveals patterns: repetitive sets of short sentences, a balance of short and longer sentences, and then ascending or descending patterns. When we have a sequence of numbers that looks as if it would bear some rhythmic fruit, we write the numbers down and the students use this prescribed set of sentence lengths to structure their written response.

Of course, this works beautifully with creative writing. As an example, here is the work of a student who I taught in 2012. She is describing a jacket to prescribed sentence lengths (27, 6, 3, 3, 3, 22, 4, 2, 1). (She was allowed some sentences longer than 20 as she is very bright, and the swearing stayed as she was 16 at the time, she was experimenting and because it kind of works.)

> The functional, workaholic jacket reflects ruefully on its past misde-meanours while sitting on a plain intelligent chair: it is grey and it is made of cheap nylon. It hangs with no shape whatsoever. It looks cheap. It smells cheap. It is cheap. Gloomy on the chair, slumped like a sloth, its lazy colour relaxes and its shape points downwards in the direction of hell. It is just shit. Utter shit. Shit.

It is easy to see how such a technique works in the area of creative writing; harder, perhaps, to see how it might work with other subjects. As an insight, I worked in an elite Australian institution for two summers running (they paid me and the people were delightful), and struggled a little with the intellectual level of the students, as they were from families who were very keen on education and had been brought up with every kind of advantage. I think I finally won them over when I asked them to write an analytical essay to prescribed sentence lengths. "Sir, this is really hard!" they'd exclaim, their handsome tanned foreheads sweating with the mental effort. "Thank God for that. I was seeing my own professional respect for myself disappearing before my eyes!" was what I didn't say. So, I'd suggest it is appropriate for other subjects too, if you have a set of kids who are up for a challenge and who have previously been seriously pretty high attainers. Just don't expect them to fly at it right away.

If you are doing creative writing with this, you can notch up the degree of difficulty and, consequently, the level of attainment a ratchet further by adding in extra instructions. If we go back to the sequence outlined above, it can present an even higher challenge if you set out the instructions like this.

Sentence 1 (3 words) – alliterative on 'D'.

Sentence 2 (3 words) – alliterative on 'B'.

Sentence 3 (3 words) – alliterative on 'D' again.

Sentence 4 (15 words) – sentence must feature two colons.

Sentence 5 (17 words) – sentence must feature a list that follows a colon.

Sentence 6 (20 words) – sentence must feature a semicolon.

Sentence 7 (1 word) – onomatopoeic!

Sentence 8 (11 words) – an animal metaphor please.

Sentence 9 (8 words) – you must get three consecutive words in this sentence to have some form of assonance on the 'I' sound.

Sentence 10 (7 words) – you must get three consecutive words in this sentence to have some form of assonance on the 'A' sound.

Sentence 11 (20 words) – try some surrealist imagery here.

Sentences 12 (one word), 13 (two words) and 14 (three words) – you must use the word you use in sentence 12 in sentences 13 and 14. Deliberate repetition for effect.

Sentence 15 (15 words) – experiment with internal rhyme here.

Sentence 16 (2 words) – consonance on 'T'.

Sentence 17 (2 words) – consonance on 'T'. Deliberate repetition for effect.

Sentence 18 (2 words) – consonance on 'T'. Deliberate repetition for effect.

As for what they write about, well, that's up to you and your imagination. But a word of advice here: almost all student work is written in the past tense: "He was walking to the shops when a man appeared." The present tense is more stylish, harder to pull off and asks them to make some quite interesting rhythmic decisions. In the present tense the previous example becomes: "He walks to the shops. A man appears." Which has more drama to it, and a staccato tension is created by the sentence length that suggests itself when the tense is changed. Oh, and on this, the present tense is far better than present continuous: "He is walking, when a man appears." I'm not sure why this is, but the present continuous is somehow less interesting and a little more childish than the present. Beware also the phrases, "He starts to ..." or "He begins to ..." These are less satisfying than "He walks"; I think, perhaps it is because the writing of these phrases feels more hesitant, less committed, so it is a stylistic tick that gets old through overuse very quickly.

NOT ENOUGH POETRY ANYWHERE EVER

When, ten years ago, the Specialist Schools and Academies Trust started propagating the clear and obvious lie that, "specialism drives up standards across the curriculum", I was working in a school with specialist technology status. Ofsted had, the same year as this status was awarded, identified the two weakest departments in the school: DT and ICT. You know what the 'T' stands for in both instances. This claim was always total drivel. (I also worked at the school whose bid for English specialism was almost entirely based on my presence in the department. I'm not sure what happened to the bid, as they sacked me for not singing the company song – which, as far as I recall, mashed up the lyrics of 'Jesus Wants Me for a Sunbeam' with those of 'Tomorrow Belongs to Me' – with the requisite blue eyed vigour.)

So, to say I've been sceptical about the notion of specialism is to understate my position, but I do remember always thinking that there would have been one specialism that, should a school ever be gifted the opportunity to offer it, would have me and Mrs Beadle knocking at their door, screaming the phrase, "Let our kids in now!" in rather too vehement a manner. What would a poetry specialism, which was based on real expertise and passion amongst the practitioners, offer to the children who were lucky enough to go to this school? Well, for a start, I don't think there would be too many literacy issues in this school, and should it be rolled out across the country, then this book would probably be entirely unnecessary. Students who were bathed in poetry on a daily basis would be more empathetic, more spiritual (in a good way), less inclined to kill each other and, crucially, versed(!) in the language at its most beautiful, with an elevated sense of what communication can be at a profound level. It would infect their speech, their thoughts and their expression. It would gift them the possibility of being songwriters whose lyrics were informed more by T. S. than by Missy. It would give them an understanding that they might, at some point, offer some pale gratitude for having lived at the same time as Leonard Cohen, before he, himself, slipped into the masterpiece. And it would endow them with the profound spiritual beauty of seeing that, whatever your conception of God, if she exists, she is to be found in the detail.

Poetry, which is language (and punctuation, or not) distilled down into its most powerful form, is whiskey for the soul: potent, colourful and transforming; it leaves traces and scars in the morning, and we do not necessarily ever recover from it. Its power is almost entirely positive: it etches itself upon us, a tattoo of language, transforming the way we see the world and the way in which we attack it. It fills us.

Aside from this, on a technical level, immersion into its grip allows us to see new things in new ways. To write a poem about a DT project may not help us construct a dovetail joint more accurately, but it will help us to understand that the only right path to take regarding our work – whatever form that work may take – is to ensure it inhabits the realm of beauty as fully as it might.

As a writer, being able to infect your prose with poetic influence transforms it: a student who deliberately constructs sentences replete with assonance has gone far beyond the factory grading function of education, and has moved into an arena where they are judged only by their own assessment of their achievements, in which external validation is no longer the teasing and unfulfilling dominatrix. "I got 11 A*s. So what? My work doesn't satisfy me as well as it might. I failed to fully nail that image and fully deserve my view of myself as being foolishness personified to the power of two."

As regards how we might do this, see the final chapter of this book.

INFECT YOUR SCHOOL
WITH POETRY

Forgive me for the fact that you might perceive this idea to be esoteric to the point of unworkable. I don't think it is.

In his years of primary school, my son, Len, only ever brought home one piece of homework that required him to do any writing or any thinking. It was a good piece of homework: nicely open ended and requiring that he involved himself in some profound thought about injustice. It was "Write a poem about war." It was the opportunity we had been waiting for, and desperate to show off that if he received homework that asked more of him than colouring in or guessing, he would show them what was in his soul, and what he was capable of. We rushed in the direction of Wikipedia and looked up the variety of poetic forms that there are (and there are lots) and decided, after a little deliberation, to write a villanelle about war.

A villanelle has nineteen lines, made up of five tercets (three line stanzas) and a final quatrain. It has two separate repetitive refrains: these hit the first and third lines of the first stanza, then alternate as the last line of the next four stanzas, until the last quatrain where they are the last two lines. As an indication of how they work, here is Len's poem:

> What a desolate thing is a man:
> His need to conquer, his requirement to rule.
> What a pitiful thing is a war.

Broken children's innocence flayed;
Broken minds flaying.
What a desolate thing is a man.

And all for the transparent water of belief
We invade, and steal; we rape and we destroy.
What a pitiful thing is a war.

My faith in what is not visible is more powerful than yours,
My culture more worthwhile.
What a desolate thing is a man.

I am more stupid than you,
And will force my understanding of wisdom onto your children and
onto your wife.
What a pitiful thing is a war.

And I will come down upon you
In a hurricane of ignorance.
What a desolate thing is a man.
What a pitiful thing is a war.

The point of this is that when teachers look at poetry across the curriculum,
we tend to reach in the direction of the ACROSTIC:

Anti-intellectual

Crass

Retarded

Obvious

Stupefying

Technique

Inculcating

Complacency in

Students

Or, if we are feeling ambitious, we might go for the haiku; hardly **an** in**t**el-ligent **k**ind of **u**ndertaking,[1] when we could be asking our students to write sonnets, terzanelles, clerihews, virelais, tankas, villanelles, rondeaus, cinquains or sestinas. We could be plastering the walls with them, and when Mrs Ofsted comes to visit, our intellectual expectations of our class would be obvious, and we wouldn't even bother filling in the literacy box, because if she couldn't see that we were working at the highest level in this class, then she shouldn't ever be allowed in a school again.

Monsieur Gove, whom we have met on a few occasions over the course of this text, was not all bad. Just disastrously arrogant. One of the ideas he came out with, and to which I initially had a really quite visceral negative reaction, was that children should be made to learn poetry by rote. He pro-posed that this would give them ownership of some form of cultural capital; that memorisation of a poem gives you access to a work of art that you own forever. Initially, I thought this to be little more than the waffling of a snob, but I've changed my mind. I've taught *Macbeth* in the region of fifteen times, and probably read it twenty times. As an accidental result of this I can recite whole scenes from memory. It is enriching to be able to do so, and I see no real reasonable rationalised objection to giving this experience to kids. The issue is, whose poetry? Answer that for yourself.

---

1   Although John Cooper Clarke's poem 'Haiku' is quite good: see http://johncooperclarke.
    com/?p=37

What would the kids get out of it, aside from being able to recall it when asked? If they are asked to perform it, and do so competitively, then they might develop skills of presentation, an innate understanding of the patterns of poetic speech, a tickle of rhetoric; to properly perform it they would have to attempt to understand how it works, and in doing so elevate both their analytical skills and their abilities as writers. I think there is a really solid argument for turning form period over to the learning of poetry, to be cemented by a big grandstand slam event each term with prizes of beautifully bound literary anthologies for the winners.

There is a volume called *Poetry by Heart* available from Penguin that might be worth a look.[2] Then again, it is recommended by the *Daily Telegraph*, so you might find that the selections are not entirely balanced in terms of representation issues. Whatever, I think that we could probably reclaim this as an idea from being perceived erroneously as the province of the right wing. Poetry is not the oppressor. Far from it. It doesn't have to be what Simon Armitage satirises as "grist for the spoken English competition, in which students at my school were expected to stand on a stage and chew their way through 'The Lady of Shalott' in a feigned and foreign RP accent".[3] It can be a bit more subversive, a bit more street, if you are going to get the kids to buy into it.

---

2   *Poetry by Heart: 200 Poems for Learning and Reciting*, intr. Andrew Motion (London: Penguin, 2014).

3   Simon Armitage, 'Poetry Should Be Subversive', *The Guardian* (12 June 2012). Available at: http://www.theguardian.com/commentisfree/2012/jun/12/poetry-should-be-subversive/.

THE SENSE OF AN ENDING[1]

When I present this work to teams of teachers, provided I've got the timings right, I will end with a plenary. As it seems somehow absurd that the author of the only serious work on the subject skips the summing up, I'll end this book in the same way I end the training: by asking you to think about the following four questions:

1   Is what you have read in any way political? Has it had political resonance? And if so, what? How will you use what you have (or haven't) learned to inform your sense of yourself as someone who teaches for social justice?

2   What has been your emotional response to what you have read? Is that response trustworthy? What have you felt most negative about? Do you still feel negative about it? Why? What, if anything, have you felt most positive about? Do you still feel positive? Why?

3   Have you learned anything about your own education, or how you can improve it? (It continues.)

4   What are you going to do differently tomorrow? Next week? Over the space of the year? What needs to change?

Now go and change things.

---

1   It is only on typing this that I finally understand it. It is the title of Julian Barnes' work after the death of his wife. Look again.

BIBLIOGRAPHY

Armitage, S. 'Poetry Should Be Subversive', *The Guardian* (12 June 2012). Available at: http://www.theguardian.com/commentisfree/2012/jun/12/poetry-should-be-subversive/.

Atwood, M. 'Falling Short: Seven Writers Reflect on Failure', *The Guardian* (22 June 2013). Available at: http://www.theguardian.com/books/2013/jun/22/falling-short-writers-reflect-failure/.

Barnes, J. *Levels of Life*. (London: Jonathan Cape, 2013).

Barnes, J. *The Sense of an Ending* (London: Jonathan Cape, 2011).

Beadle, P. *How to Teach* (Carmarthen: Crown House Publishing, 2010).

Beadle, P. *Literacy through Football Skills* (Carmarthen: Crown House Publishing, 2009).

Black, P. and Wiliam, D. 'Assessment and Classroom Learning', *Assessment in Education* 5(1) (1998).

Bull, B. L. and Wittrock, M. C. 'Imagery in the Learning of Verbal Definitions', *British Journal of Educational Psychology* 43(3) (1973).

Crystal, D. *Spell It Out: The Singular Story of English Spelling* (London: Profile, 2012).

Department for Children, Schools and Families *Support for Spelling. The National Strategies: Primary* (London: DCSF, 2010).

Didau, D. *The Secret of Literacy: Making the Implicit, Explicit* (Carmarthen: Independent Thinking Press, 2014).

Dixon, J. *Growth through English: A Report Based on the Dartmouth Seminar 1966* (Reading: National Association for the Teaching of English, 1969).

Dolch, E. W. *Problems in Reading* (Champaign, IL: Garrard Press, 1948).

Eide, D. *The Dolch List Explained: Sounding Out the Sight Words* (Minneapolis: Pedia Learning Inc., 2013).

Gilbert, I. *The Little Book of Thunks: 260 Questions to Make Your Brain Go Ouch!* (Carmarthen: Crown House Publishing, 2007).

Gill, A. A. 'Table Talk: Brasserie Chavot, London, W1', *Sunday Times Magazine* (2 June 2013).

Hitchens, C. *God is not Great: The Case against Religion* (London: Atlantic Books, 2007).

Jenkins, S. 'Cameron Has Failed to Resist the Lunchtime Lobbyists' Lure', *The Guardian* (19 July 2014). Available at: http://www.theguardian.com/commentisfree/2013/jul/18/lobbying-buying-influence-taints-politics/.

Kamm, O. 'Plain English Baloney II' (24 March 2004). Available at: http://oliverkamm.typepad.com/blog/2004/03/plain_english_b.html/.

Klein, C. and Millar, R. R. *Unscrambling Spelling* (London: Hodder & Stoughton, 1990).

Motion, A. (intr.) *Poetry by Heart: 200 Poems for Learning and Reciting*, (London: Penguin, 2014).

Paivio, A. *Imagery and Verbal Processes* (New York: Holt, Rinehart, and Winston, 1971).

Pinker, S. '10 "Grammar Rules" It's OK to Break (Sometimes)', *The Guardian* (15 August 2014). Available at: http://www.theguardian.com/books/2014/aug/15/steven-pinker-10-grammar-rules-break/.

Tiley-Nunn, N. *How to Teach: Primary Maths* (Carmarthen: Crown House Publishing, 2014).

Truss, L. *Eats, Shoots & Leaves: The Zero Tolerance Approach to Punctuation* (London: Profile Books, 2003).

United Nations, Secretary-General Stresses Need for Political Will and Resources to Meet Challenge of Fight against Illiteracy (press release, 8 September 1997). Available at: http://www.un.org/press/en/1997/19970904.SGSM6316.html/.

Willis, P. *Learning to Labor: How Working Class Kids Get Working Class Jobs* (New York: Columbia University Press, 1977).

Wilson, G. *Breaking through Barriers to Boys' Achievement: Developing a Caring Masculinity* (London: Network Continuum, 2008).

INDEX

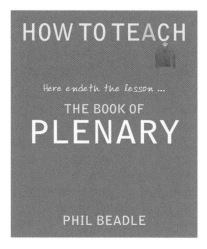

HOW TO TEACH

Here endeth the lesson ...

THE BOOK OF
PLENARY

PHIL BEADLE

ISBN 978-178135053-9

The 'How to Teach' series covers every element of classroom practice
in a highly practical, but wildly irreverent, manner.

independentthinkingpress.com

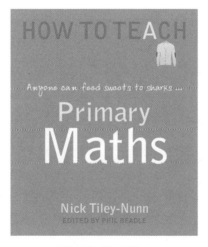

ISBN 978-178135135-2

The 'How to Teach' series covers every element of classroom practice
in a highly practical, but wildly irreverent, manner.

independentthinkingpress.com

PHIL BEADLE

HOW TO
TEACH

provokes, at times shocks, but above all teaches   controversial
readable, hugely readable   necessary, hugely necessary   irreverent
hip, sharp, sussed, funny and extremely practical   hilarious
a scintillating, pedagogical romp   intoxicating, deeply wise
laugh-out-loud, embarrass-yourself-in-public funny

ISBN 978-184590393-0

The 'How to Teach' series covers every element of classroom practice
in a highly practical, but wildly irreverent, manner.

independentthinkingpress.com